INERTIA

a novel

INERTIA

a novel

Kim Cope Tait

Conversations with Crows Press
New Zealand
www.cwcpress.com

Conversations with Crows Press
New Zealand
www.kimcopetait.com

INERTIA

CWC Press books may be purchased for educational, business, or sales promotional use. For information address the author via the website: www.kimcopetait.com.

Third Edition

ISBN Number: 978-1-944242-32-9

…for Danielle Martin
in loving memory

ACKNOWLEDGMENTS

Dwaine, my beloved, for letting me be the thing that I am, unwieldy kite in your blue sky.

Rakai and Taiaroa for choosing me. I am so ed, my loves.

The midwives of this work: Basia Wasowski, Andrea Weimer and Betsy Boland.

Maridel Salisbury for being the mother whose love and grief raised the first question in my heart at the age of 18. Your boy will always be here.

Mary Pat Akers, to whose son Spencer the first production of *Inertia* the stage play was dedicated. He is our snow angel, always.

Liz Morriss and Kris Martin, whose babies blessed me infinitely and then, went gently on their way.

Carolyn Swanson for understanding just what this work has meant for me.

Noe Erger for sharing your art with me for *Inertia*'s first garment. I love you, sister.

Meghann Schroers for reserving judgment until I asked you not to.

Debi Wraga for falling in love with *Inertia* "at first sight" and believing immediately in its life.

The original cast and crew of *Inertia* the stage play: Robert Dean, Ashley Lowes, Sarah Hara, Kristen Kesonen, Nica Mayer, Annikka Thomas, Alex Canning, Jake Fulton, Anna Gainey, Evan Thomas, Janae Anderson, Rory Thost, Joe Zalan, Camille Betts, Anna Squire, Mattias Horseman, Marija Yelizarova, Jayan Fazal,

Justin Cornett and Paul Vurst. Also, the singers and musicians: Abdullah Khan, Meghan Hooper, Samantha Beckett, Hazal Uzunkaya, Ian Yeats, Jake Cassman and Michael Vacas. Your embodiment of my script truly helped to inspire the shape that *Inertia* the novel took on in the course of its creation.

Finally, Mom and Dad for the love and support of your poet daughter.

My profound gratitude to all of you…

PROLOGUE

Jake

It wasn't Angela's fault. I knew that. There was nothing to forgive. And yet there was some little cruelty in me that would not allow me to approach her that day. As if doing so might shift something that was precariously balanced by my isolated grief. As if approaching her there, in the Chapel of the Four Seasons, sharing what grieved us both, might begin to close a wound I was not finished with. One I was still nursing attentively. It is so clear to me now, what I might have done to ease Angela's suffering, if I could have lifted myself out of my own, even for a moment. Such is hindsight. Such is our generosity in retrospect. I see now that spirit will give anything; it is the body, the frail and self-indulgent "mortal coil," that refuses itself. Cannot give away.

Angela

It wasn't my fault. It was never my fault, and I think I always knew that, somewhere in my tangled consciousness. But this is not the beginning. I think that trying to find the beginning of anything seems somehow misdirected in this cyclical life. Either your motion is carrying you forward, or you are somewhere above the ground, spinning and perhaps just out of reach, not in contact with anything that could provide traction and create forward momentum. But I spin a web of words again, and this is meant to be a story. It is a story about angels and inertia. It is a story about self, hovering or otherwise, and it is a story about the business of soul mates.

Everyone has their own idea about soul mates, and some reject the idea entirely. Personally, I think we have many. And I think there is what we like to refer to as 'the one.' The pressure to identify 'the one' is great; and the uncertainty around that identification is equally great, sometimes even once it has been made. I speak with dubious authority, I know, but I have known three angels in my life, and I have loved one man. Really loved him. Since I was only a girl. These four entities taught me what a soul mate is. They taught me patience and grace. They taught me love.

PART ONE

Spring 1989

One

Angela

Lake Tulloch is a man-made reservoir tucked in the hills of the San Joaquin Valley in Northern California. In the spring, the hills are still a pale green, and the lake usually quite full with cool runoff from the Sierra Nevadas. What I remember most about the lake is the scent of the spear grass in the morning, or after a rain, and the whisper of shoreline breezes through its thin stalks. Yellow, toasted by the sun and bearing thousands of the much-maligned foxtails that function as tiny rattles, airy wind chimes, the spear grass moves in waves. It makes a perfect nest for a sleeping dog under an oak tree and fills the air with an organic, heavy kind of odor that is as much California to me as any other phenomenon. It is more like grain than grass, more redolent of wheat than lawn in its hearty fragrance.

You can smell the spear grass on the way to the lake along Route 152, where cars rise slowly above the apple orchards of Oakdale, nearing Tuolumne County. The passing orchards framed by my car window would mesmerize me, as my eyes flicked between following now-horizontal, now-diagonal rows of blossoming trees, their tiny white petals dusting the earth like snow.

Passing Lover's Leap indicates that you are nearly there. I remember imagining up the two teenagers said to have been impelled to take their own lives, hand in hand, from this knob of hardened greenstone. They would have leapt out over oak forests and the golden spear grass below, all of it punctuated by cascading, lichen-covered stones. What desperation. What ardor. Fearlessness, I thought. They must have been two whose entire scope of awareness had closed in on one another, admitting nothing beyond their own singular gazes. *Not even to have hesitated on the brim of certain death*—or perhaps they did stall. To kiss each other again. To console each other about mothers forsaken, brothers abandoned—and then leapt without even taking a breath. Perhaps they held each other tightly. Or sailed out over the cliff, fingers loosely entwined, that their spirits might disengage from their bodies unhindered.

With eyes closed and spear grass still swirling in my nostrils, I could see their ghosts join one another in the air above flesh and bone crushed under the weight of earth's gravitational pull, augmented by hundreds of feet of vertical landscape. Stones and spear grass had passed rapidly up and up, their bodies down and down. I was a dreamer, and this was one of the dreams that repeated itself each time I passed this particular stretch of highway on the way to the lake or home again. The faces of the lovers morphed into different people then and have done so since, in waking dreams, but there is always spear grass. There is always stone.

When the gang arrived in Kenya's van on Sunday morning, all of them sweaty and hot and laughing even though her heater lever was stuck in the 'on' position for three quarters of the way to our lake house, I felt great relief. I think maybe I had secretly thought they might not show. Not that I feared they would disappoint me; that would not have occurred to me. But that some accident might prevent them from coming: a flat tire, a family emergency, an overturned fuel truck on the highway.

Now they just poured themselves out of the sliding door and into the lake water, immediately relieved and giggling. I remember the image of their doffed rubber slippers dotting the water fully. The twins, Sam and Kenya, bird-boned beauties, were already golden-skinned on that early spring weekend. Their blond hair fanned around their heads in the water like halos, like lions' manes, like sunlight.

Athena and Jake bantered and exulted quietly in the new shape of their relationship to one another, which now included furtive little kisses and letting their fingers glide in and out of the other's hands or hair. She appeared to me then as the young goddess for whom she was named, not birthed like a mere mortal, but having sprung from her father's mind, fully armored and ready for battle. 'Clear-eyed,' with hair slick as crow feathers and as black, she was so lovely it hurt.

We played in the lake all day under the approving gazes of my parents, who were undeniably relieved themselves to see that I was socializing normally. That in fact home schooling and carting me around the world for the better part of my childhood to photograph the more ordinary lives of others had not damaged me irrevocably, nor rendered me socially incompetent.

They looked at these four youths as little saviors, answers to prayers they hadn't the belief system to support, and my dad drove the boat tirelessly for us to ride behind on various buoyant apparatus. My favorite was the giant yellow inner tube, which was yanked around at wild speeds behind the boat, one or two of us clinging fervently to the handles and laughing madly in an effort to stay on. Invariably my dad won the game, which was simply to knock us off, at which time our bodies would skip crazily across the water before sinking only enough for our heads to bob between the orange arches of our life vests.

It was the shared eighteenth birthday of the three

girls, and all day we were sharing thoughts about the 'future,' what that might look like, what it might contain for each of us in our striving. I had such vast plans for those years and the years beyond. I wanted to study philosophy, become the conduit of human pondering in service of the only legitimate goal in life: to seek truth. I thought that all other virtues would follow. Even beauty, I believed, was bereft of its meaning without the existence of truth; at its most extreme, this Keatsian view defined beauty as truth's physical manifestation, thereby rendering beauty nonexistent in the shadow of lies or deceit. It's why we are so drawn to beauty, I thought: we are relentlessly thirsty for the true, the real and finally, the beautiful.

I had energy for everything academic, everything organic; I had chosen my university for its proximity to the sea and for the accomplishment of its philosophy department. I believed in the limitlessness of human potential, though I wasn't sure about God. I, who had been raised by parents who called themselves, only half-jokingly, pagans, could not divorce myself from a very pragmatic sense of the truth I so revered and sought in every atom, every interaction, every syllable of language I heard. I speak of this belief system, or its loose architecture, in the past tense not because it no longer exists, but because it exists now in a different configuration, having undergone an immense and explosive rearrangement over the course of slow-moving time.

But I get ahead of myself. The web of words begins to overwhelm the story; my desperate language in the foreground; what aches, what saves, sliding into position as backdrop. I pull it to the fore again. One cannot truly live within a poem. One does not truly spring from the mind like a goddess but is birthed, messy, bloody, flesh and bone. One cannot contrive to live only in the mind, even if this seems the safest measure against the real. This I know. The memory is always immediate, Techni, alive:

I am driving the boat. I have coaxed the keys from my reluctant but smiling father, kissed his forehead and heeded my mother's advice to grab a sweater. It can be chilly on the water at night, and the sun has just set on a day that seemed perfect. A day that saw me as the fullest human being I had yet embodied, a day that garnered me with friends, meant freedom from fear.

"Ahhhh," Jake had exclaimed when I produced a cooler of beer upon leaving the cove and entering open water. "You're the best, Angela," and to the others: "Let's keep her." We had all laughed at this, but it felt very real to me, this innocent proclamation. Yes, they intended to keep me. I was no longer a stray.

I am driving the boat. The gurgle of the jet engine is like a low growl, as we move across the water, glossy and smooth as a mirror. I anticipate the reflection of stars only beginning to emerge. I breathe in the dry chaparral air, one hand on the throttle.

Jake and Athena are nestled in each other's arms, sipping a shared Corona. We move slowly through black water, Kenya's soft soprano sliding through the air about our ears, as she sings:

"Give me these moments back. Give them back to me." It is a Kate Bush song I know well now. One that has echoed in my head at intervals for two decades. My conception of it has reconfigured itself in as many ways as the image of the lovers leaping from their craggy peak behind my eyelids; in as many ways as memory itself; in as many ways as the body of what I think I know, what I think I believe.

"Give me that little kiss," Kenya croons, "give me your hand."

Sam lies back on the seat in front of me, her damp hair fanned out across the white marine cushion. She is listening to Kenya, too, basking in the glow of a salad bowl moon. The shoreline is dotted with campfires on the south end, the soft sound of voices and the faint scent of smoky mesquite drifting out over the water occasionally. There is no wind tonight. I would remember that. I would remember if the spear grass had been singing. I would remember if the air had been moving the trees along the ridge.

There is a moment that feels like we are in a vacuum. There is no sound, and this I know as a fault of my recollection. Surely there is the sound of a jet engine racing toward us from within the cove. Surely there are human voices uttering their surprise, their simultaneous wonder at a boat appearing from thin air. But I hear nothing. I am frozen. Jake stands, half lifting Athena with him. Her eyes are discs, her mouth a small "o." We are nothing. We are molecules against sky, we are — light—flesh and bone—we are bodies in air, under water, tangled with fiberglass and steel. We are wrapped in bubbles, turbulence, jetsam. We are all of these. We are lost to one another. We are fire, the collision that rends us from ourselves. We are gone.

Two

Angela

My life with Athena, Kenya, Sam and Jake, a relatively brief period (34 days I later calculated), was protracted and replayed like a disjointed film in the soft nest of my unconsciousness. It was like the incubation of my equanimity, a warm pocket of time that insulated me from the terror of waking and what would be required of me afterward. It was an indulgence to let my body lie motionless, apparently lifeless, while my mind traveled with my friends through our shared experience. With any volition, I think I would have remained there, separated from my broken body, forever.

My visions in this state, drifting among degrees of un/consciousness, were not like ordinary memories. Every word was crisp, every gesture. Not like I usually remember things. Movies I remember in impressions. No matter how many times I see a film, my memory of it is like a Monet painting…or a Cezanne, depending on the genre. Sometimes all I can muster is a Jackson Pollock. My memory of experience is usually the same: I carry with me only the sensations it gave me, the general outline of its content, the essential s that strained my sensibility in the moments I took it in. I don't remember dialogue or specific action. Only shapes and impressions. These *vision-memories* are not like that. They are crystalline. I can play them back again and again, as if the reel exists in my head and I have only to push 'play.'

Day 1: Tuesday March 14, 1989

The first day I remember meeting them, I was at the Yogurt Shack on 41st Avenue. It was a fishbowl of a yogurt and smoothie bar, inside of which people moved silently beneath neon signage. From the busy street outside, they appeared like aquatic creatures, adorned in light and lumbering among wire-backed chairs across white tiles. They all clutched nonfat yogurts heaped with crushed candy bars or cookie dough, served up to them by the luminous Jake and Athena. They wore the requisite pink hats and lime-green ties and greeted each customer with mischievous grins. I was fidgeting at the counter and had ordered my usual: nonfat vanilla with Oreo cookies.

The Oreo cookies were running low, and Jake rather obsequiously offered to get more from the cabinet behind them. I remember Athena flushing slightly as Jake bent low, nearly half of his bare buttocks exposed to the 'incorporeal air.' He had hiked his pants down in the tradition of the best of the best 'plumber's cracks,' and Athena stifled her laughter as she tried to block him from view with her own thin frame. I felt myself blushing, too, and took the change she was handing me with a rather apologetic look on her face.

I took a seat outside on the little patio with my Golden Retriever Grimace at one of the café tables. I took slow bites of my yogurt, watching them between chapters of *The Mists of Avalon*. Athena's hair was black and did that shifty thing admired by girls with straight and curly hair alike. It was layered around her face and fell almost to the small of her back. As always, she wore about a hundred of those little black rubber bracelets and donned heavy black eyeliner. Her Doc Marten shoes were offset by a flouncy, long skirt with leggings and two or three lacy little tops layered in the post-"Like a Virgin" style. She looked fairly ridiculous in her pink hat at work, but the way she wore it without a grain of self-consciousness—I decided then that this must have been one of the things Jake found most beautiful in her.

I could see even then that they were in love, though they themselves were only beginning to discover it. Jake's floppy hair was out of his grey-green eyes for a change that day, beneath the pineapple-logo hat. It was the same shade of sea kelp as mine, but his skin was the of caramel, while mine was fair and endowed with a substantial number of fine freckles, my nose perennially peeling.

He was taller than Athena by at least six inches, and the way he leaned into her, over her, was tree-like, gentle, as they spoke in hushed tones. Then they would erupt again into farcical antics that rippled out in waves of laughter and broke into the air. Their tide just reached me, its susurrus swirling around my ankles and receding again into the vast reservoir of their affection.

I was still sitting outside with Grimace when Kenya and Sam rolled up in Kenya's bright green VW bus. Pato Banton was mid-howl from stock speakers when she turned the key and the engine made its few final rotations, settled into the 'off' mode. The bus windows were adorned with pink and orange bathtub stickers, and a silver peace symbol on a beaded cord swung rather wildly from the rearview mirror, still reeling from Kenya's quick turn into the parking stall.

I saw them stop before getting out, watching through the windshield: Jake and Athena in reversed roles this time, Jake screening Athena's ridiculously exposed behind from their newest customer. While Jake received two dollars fifty from the pudgy hands of a middle-aged woman in spandex tights and an oversized sweatshirt,

Athena foraged deliberately in the low cupboards behind them, pretending not to be able to locate the extra rainbow sprinkles. When the scene ended and the woman departed, licking her rainbow sprinkled yogurt with great relish, Kenya and Sam burst in like wind or another ocean wave breaking over damp stones. Their chatter was contagious, their energy delicious.

"Are you still playing the butt crack game?" teased Sam, who was wearing Lighthouse High's red and gold swim team parka, her hair still wet from the pool. Her standard checkered slip-on Vans and Levi's 501's were visible beneath the gold piping of the jacket. "Gross."

"I think I win," Athena said to Jake, grinning, "Do I win?" It was as much a statement as a question.

"Hands down," he said, knitting his eyebrows together in mock seriousness. He cocked his head significantly downward to meet her eyes.

"Grow up!" chided Kenya, and Jake and Athena broke again into ridiculous laughter, wound up dishtowels with which to snap each other.

"We on for Saturday night?" Jake asked, pausing only briefly in his towel-snapping.

"Ouch!" cried Sam, receiving a deft towel snap to the derriere, delivered by Athena. "Day after the big meet! Where's the party?" she said.

"The Point…Sarena's house on the cliffs. We'll celebrate your victory. It's gonna' be huge!" Jake said.

"'Course we're on!" chimed Kenya, "and of course she's going to win." They were talking about the upcoming Santa Cruz County League Championships for swimming and diving. Sam was our star diver, I our school newspaper's lead photographer for the event.

"Pick you up at seven. Barbecue, bonfire, the works. I offered to bring firewood," said Kenya.

"So I'm humping firewood to the party," Jake complained. I flipped the page in my book, though I'd not been reading at all. Grimace gave me a look that made me feel foolish and guilty at once, then started panting again in the warm air around our heads.

"Just doing our part!" Kenya said unapologetically.

"Nice hat," she said to Jake, flicking the brim with her index finger as he prepared her chocolate yogurt.

"Shut up," he said, jerking his head back in mild annoyance, hands too busy to retaliate.

"No, I mean it," she continued, persisting in trying to reach it over the glass shield of the counter as he scooped fresh strawberries onto her full-fat dessert. When he turned his head to the side, she began flicking his ear softly with the tips of her fingers.

"Piss off, man!" he growled, a hint of a smile presenting itself at the edges of his mouth, even as he dodged her flitting hand and arranged her spoon and lid. Her vast smile meant her teasing forgiven instantly, his infinite patience with her under any circumstance.

Looking around, Kenya shifted gears. "So they call in the lackeys for the busy shifts, huh?" she said. I noticed then that the only occupied table was mine, and as if her comment had suddenly revealed me for the voyeur I was, I quickly gathered up my book, Grimace's leash and my half-eaten yogurt to vacate my table. As I walked back toward Pleasure Point, where I had parked my car, their easy chatter followed me until I was out of the range of hearing. I considered the easy way these four luminous creatures had with each other. I had befriended Capuchin monkeys in the jungles of Costa Rica, but this…how to be so comfortable in one's skin and in the company of peers?

I fed the second half of my soupy yogurt to Grimace when I got to the Hook and stood watching the waves for a bit. The open ends of the little barrels reminded me of cauliflower, and I watched them roll in, one after another. I would surf glass off at Sewers, my favorite weekday evening activity. I would paddle out in five millimeters of neoprene, pull my way through sea kelp and foam with cold-numbed hands, until the sun no longer lit the bay.

In the water, I was fish-like, slippery and limitless,

sans the wire-rimmed glasses I relied on in those days to see when I was on land. In the sea I could feel my way, follow shadow and movement without having to identify specifics. Riding waves was about patterns, intuition, momentum. Nothing you had to focus on with your eyes.

Day 4: Friday March 17, 1989

Only a few days later came the day of the SCCAL Swimming and Diving Championships. Our school, Lighthouse High, was hosting that year, and I was 'on assignment.' It was sunny but unusually cold, even for March, and a fine steam rose from the bodies of the swimmers and divers as they left the water and their skin hit the frigid air. I was taking photographs for the Lighthouse Sentinel, limning the edges of the scene as usual and separated from the action by multiple lenses: those of the camera and those of my glasses.

I remember Sam standing on the cement pool deck near the diving board, as the scores from the previous diver were announced and the crowd applauded. Sam appeared to be completely unaware of the host of people watching her, or even of any of the other divers, though their nervous anticipation of her next dive pervaded the air. Her eyes were closed as she visualized her dive and ran through a vigorous charade; it suggested that what followed would involve spinning in a tight ball and the explosion of limbs into a taut, arrow-shaped, head-first entry into the water.

"Next up is Samantha Hawthorne, a senior at Lighthouse High. She is the current record-holder for the SCCAL district and reigning SCCAL champion. Her final dive will be a back one and one half somersault, degree of difficulty, 2.2."

Sam ran a pink Sammy quickly over keenly muscled arms and legs and took her place on the diving board. I moved silently around the periphery, shooting photos of her there against the sky. Her ribcage expanded to receive the air she drew in silkily, and then—her approach.

I thought that I had caught her with my camera, but I wouldn't be sure until later in the darkroom. There was almost no splash, and it was over. Sam came up smiling broadly and was immediately enveloped by her friends and her coach. Kenya tousled Sam's hair and wiped a smudge of mascara from under her eye, while I clicked away from my distance. They were all thrilled, Jake and Athena exchanging high-fives and celebrating Sam's victory already. They quickly settled down as the announcer began to give the scores.

"Eight, seven and one half, eight, seven, eight and one half." Sam's face was incredulous, tears forming over their glossy azul, as the crowd erupted into cheers. She had won again. She would leave her high school years with a medal around her neck, her name etched on a vast sign above the pool deck that recognizes record-holding athletes.

Day 5: Saturday March 18, 1989

The sun had already set when, dripping wet, I climbed the rocks at the Point, every finger and toe numb but every pore of my skin tingling with the post-surf sensation that invigorates for an hour after a session and then lulls us gently into sleep if we acquiesce to it. I was contemplating this sensation and the way my surfboard felt in my icy hands, when I suddenly found myself encircled by some boys from school.

Without my glasses, it took me a moment, but I recognized Marco Sanders from my Economics class; the others were only vaguely familiar as the two shapes that flanked him whenever I passed him in the halls.

I remember noticing the whispery orange glow of the sky behind the little market at the corner, now long closed, and how quiet the street felt. It was the time between the busy-ness of the day and the activity of the night, when the last surfers emerge from the water like glossy black seals and only become human as they approach and what light is left defines them. These new figures, though blurry in my vision, were in stark contrast to that comfortable scene, and having to acknowledge them was more of an annoyance to me at first.

It was Marco who spoke: "Look at this, guys!" With that he took my surfboard out of my hands and with one quick jab knocked my middle fin off on one of the wooden posts skirting the Point. I was speechless, and annoyance quickly escalated to alarm. Wheeling around on me, Marco began to survey me, head to foot. In my myopic haze, I imagined him leering, licking his lips, maybe, like a dog.

"Not so homely without the glasses. And where's the hat?" He handed the board to one of the other boys and reached for my hair. This time I reacted and moved away from him, but still tentative, fearful. Even in that moment I remember feeling frustrated by my own timorous demeanor.

"Let me smell it," Marco persisted, this time successful in taking a handful of my hair and pressing it to his face. I could feel the other two getting a little uncomfortable as Marco swiped at the cord attached to the zipper of my wetsuit. "Got a bikini under there?" he spat.

"Let's go, you guys," said the kid now holding my board, nervously shifting its weight in his arms. He wore a white beanie and a white sweatshirt that seemed to blend with my surfboard in the blur of the things I perceived. Absurdly, I remember thinking that he resembled the Stay-Puff Marshmallow Man, but the comedy of this image was eclipsed by my fear and by Marco's hot breath way too near my face.

"No, I want to get to know this girl. She's been hiding." And before I could really sort out Marco's intentions, I heard Kenya's voice, deliberately loud, behind me.

"What's up, guys?"

"Get lost, Kenya. Don't you have some small population of sea otters to save? A rainforest maybe?" Marco sneered at her. His goons seemed to like this and they chortled a bit.

"I'm off the clock," she said coolly, turning toward me then. "Angela, right?" Shocked and relieved at once, I nodded.

"Come on, Angela," she said casually and turning to the boys she added, "She was just coming to meet us." Athena and Sam had caught up with Kenya by now and were standing with us. Sam took my surfboard out of the hands of the Stay-Puff kid, who let it go but whispered under his breath.

"Bitch."

"Excuse me?" Sam practically yelled, "I know you did not just call me a bitch, you reprobate."

"That's 'Sam' for dickhead," said Athena, as if he needed a translator. I was blinking, trying to bring the picture into focus, which I knew was an exercise in futility but continued to do anyway.

Just then, Jake walked up with an armload of firewood. "Hey, what's up?" he asked warily, quickly taking in the scene: the agitated expressions of the three boys, the combative stance of Kenya and Sam. Me, standing there in a little puddle of salt water. "Is there a problem here?"

"Piss off, Jake," said Marco between clenched jaws.

"We were just leaving," said Athena discreetly as she essentially herded me away from the little circle and toward the cars lined along the road.

"Yeah, Marco and his boys were just entertaining our new friend. Thanks guys, we've got it from here." Kenya's sarcasm was controlled, her tone deftly toeing the line between rendering humiliation and inciting rage. Marco found himself wordless and, blustering something about a 'waste of time,' led his buddies away from us into the quickly descending night.

At my car, a white Volkswagen Rabbit I had bought for fifteen hundred dollars from a , complete with diesel engine and an eight-track stereo, archaic even for 1989, I began making a quick "deck change" into my jeans. From the passenger's seat, out came the glasses and the ball cap, and a look of vague recollection passed across Jake's face finally. I had seen him around, but I was pretty sure he had never seen me. When he finally spoke, he was a bit cross but ever with that quality of being willing to forgive almost anything in these three beauties.

"You trying to get me killed?" he whined.

"You?" Sam said, incredulously.

"Yeah, me! I'm going to get killed hanging out with you guys. They're not going to kick *your* ass!"

"Oh, come on. You could take 'em, Jake!" teased Kenya, circling him now with her fists raised comically. Jake looked at Kenya in disbelief but also obvious affection.

"Shit," he said under his breath and headed again toward the houses along the cliffs, the girls all laughing at him gently, Athena mussing his hair as he passed. We watched him go, as if anticipating his stop to ask, "You guys coming, or are you going to stay on the street and pick fights?"

There was a general movement in his direction and Athena turned to me, inconceivably, and asked, "Wanna' come?" I did. More than anything.

"Uh, to Sarena Wilson's party?" I asked. Kenya understood the implication of my question immediately. Sarena was a 'betty,' one of the volleyball team girls whose lip gloss glazed the tops of peach wine cooler bottles at every weekend party. I had never been invited into the society of such creatures, let alone transcended its exclusivity the way Kenya, Sam and Athena had.

"Yeah, you're our guest," she said, putting her arm lightly over my shoulder.

"Yeah," I said, "okay." And we were off.

When I walked into Sarena Wilson's party, something stirred in me, ever so slightly, and I was intrigued by the casual atmosphere of social mingling, the posturing of the opposing genders over keg cups, or those clear plastic ones with the strawberries bobbing around inside. I could see that there was an art to almost every aspect of this scene, from the movement of a girl's hand through her hair to the ribald banter and subsequent mini-wrestling match between two athletic senior boys. Sarena Wilson's disdainful glance had in it, too, a sort of choreography, as well as the way she shifted her drink to her right hand and slinked over to us with the fabric of her denim mini-skirt pressed between her left hand and her hip.

"Hey Kenya! Athena, Sam." The omission of my name was no mistake and I did not take it for one. My cheeks burned, but I held my ground, surrounded as I was by the three girls I knew to move with freedom among the various cliques at Lighthouse High. They were not bound by these artificial barriers; tonight I wouldn't be either. Sarena was wearing her cheerleader sweater and gold lamé pumps with white ankle socks, the kind little girls wear to first communion. I quietly admired the way she walked over lawn and landscaping slate skillfully, as if her high heels were extensions of her feet and she some sort of glamorous mountain goat.

"Hey, Sarena. This is Angela. Angela, Sarena," said Kenya without missing a beat. She glanced casually over our heads toward the sea, as Sarena shook my hand gingerly, surveying me in an instant. Here, the ocean knocked at one's door all day long and silently threatened to disintegrate, over many years perhaps, the very ground upon which one's house was built. I was still contemplating that and Sarena's caprine agility on heels when she addressed me.

"Nice to meet you, Angela," said Sarena civilly, though she was already noticing the three jersey-clad football players entering at the gate, two of which bore a beer keg on their shoulders. Just as quickly as I had gained Sarena's disfavor, I had lost her attention, and the little tension bubble that was barely forming had already popped. I felt relieved almost at once.

"Great party," I managed to utter weakly as she whisked herself away in a cloud of Dior Poison perfume. I was pretty sure she didn't hear me.

"Grab a brew!" she called back to us over her shoulder and having dumped her little cup had both hands free to deliver hugs and kisses to the arriving males, to exclaim over the strength that must be required to carry such a heavy thing, to gesticulate about this thing and that under their adoring gazes. I watched the whole scene with interest.

Physically unthreatening, usurping none of the male attention designated to Sarena and her friends, I was able to slip back into my head, comfortable with my own relative invisibility. I picked my way through the crowd, following Sam and basking in my real, albeit contrived, initiation into Lighthouse High social life.

Sam did not know and could not have guessed that the beer she handed me that night in the red keg cup was my first, and she gave it to me without hesitation, like we were at the dinner table and she was handing me the salt shaker. Bumping my hip with hers she gave me a small wrinkle of her nose, too, which suggested a secret that we shared. It was like that. Easy. Comfortable. I drank the beer in tiny sips and enjoyed the bubbles that seemed to escape to my nose every time I swallowed. Mostly I followed Sam around, or Athena, and kept quiet.

We eventually found our way to a sofa that had been dragged out of Sarena's house and onto the rocks. It was turned to face the sea, where floodlights were now illuminating the heavy waves rising there. They were curling into long barrels and spitting whitewater from their cavernous bellies. Some of the surfer boys from school were stripping down in the sandy cove below us, and the light reflected off white rear ends as they strapped on their leashes and laughing, streaked out into the water for a full-moon surf.

Much later, it seemed, a girl's voice increased its treble by degrees, and I saw that a boy twice her size and equally drunk was trying to bury his face in her neck. With his free hand he was grappling clumsily with the hem of her skirt. Someone was vomiting in a planter, the greasy locks of his rockabilly hairdo springing from its shellacked position haphazardly.

A circle of girls with shoulder-padded blouses and wide, low-slung belts appeared to me like back-up singers for the Thompson Twins, their giant hair frothing all around their smudgy faces. Instead of singing into a microphone, they were taking turns catching a foaming stream of beer from a hole punched with a key in the bottom of a can. They laughed as the beer overflowed their open mouths and dripped down their chins. I looked back as we left the party, with this distinct impression of them: lip-sticked fledglings awaiting nourishment, shocked by the forcefulness with which it arrived.

We rather scrambled back to Kenya's van, "Flower Power," as she liked to call it, laughing and experiencing the night the way one does with a good buzz on…a little muffled, a little unsteady, and adorned with an elusive glossiness that shimmers over things unexpectedly and then reappears without warning. I felt a little behind that shimmer most of the night but was perfectly content to be there; it was like a game, and chasing that shimmer, I remember being delighted, amused by the unexpected freedom under which I was operating.

Day 10: Friday March 23, 1989

About a week later, I was surfing a clean left-hander

at Davenport. Davenport, several miles north of Santa Cruz, had been my new home since August, when my traveling parents had finally touched down after fifteen years of photographing the people and places of the world, their little girl in tow.

I had left my worries on the beach after another day spent completely alone, though surrounded by the throngs of teenagers that populated Lighthouse High. The fact that I had ridden camels in Egypt, spent days haunting the periphery of an ashram in India and stood in the square where Marie Antoinette was executed in Paris, ironically, made me nothing but a foreigner in my new milieu, where localism thrived with inconceivable strength. For now, I was completely free of the tension that buzzed up and down my spine on an average day at school.

As I sat straddling my surfboard and scanning the horizon for change, my hands tucked under my armpits for warmth, I let my mind roam to my new friends, and particularly to Jake.

Jake seemed just about perfect to me in those days. He was extremely smart, I knew, having exhausted all the English courses at Lighthouse, which meant that he had to have challenged Freshman English. He was enrolled this year in poetry and literature classes at Cortez College and was acing them all, or so I had heard girls whisper as he passed in the halls. They whispered about other things, too, of course, but I was most impressed by this. I had always been a fool for a boy who could manage language into poetry. A boy who could move me with his words.

Out in the water that day, I imagined Jake as a young Keats, though I had never read a single syllable written by him, and I was the more enamored. I remember sitting there on my board, watching for bumps on the thin line that separated the sky from the sea, spinning my board around and paddling for the ones with most promise. I was thinking of Jake in his shiny black Ray Bans, his eyes all but invisible behind their dark green lenses, evoking Bryan Adams and all the affection in my teenage heart.

I remember one ride in particular that afternoon, inextricably linked as it was with a particular line of thought. I remember feeling the lift of the wave as it dragged itself over the reef deep below me, pitched itself skyward and sent me skittering down its glossy face. Some waves are like this. Exponentially memorable. The pedestal I had constructed around Jake's feet had all but forced the Jake Jameson in my imagination to step onto it, to accommodate what I believed, for no good reason, to be true of him. I remember shifting my weight to the back of my board then, knowing that this would slow my forward momentum and place me in the pit of the wave. I knew I would not make it out of the barrel, but I relished in the moment, dragged my left hand in the glossy wall of water that enclosed me. Jake would have many years to grow into the version of himself that I envisioned, but I had lost the thread of this thought and dove into the back of the wave, held tight to my knees, was throttled by its breaking turbulence.

When my head broke the surface, aching with the cold, it had all been worth it. I shook the boy from my hair and paddled back into the lineup. I had no understanding then that Jake Jameson was light years away from embodying the man I had dreamed up, or perhaps intuited. It mattered little that he loved Athena, who, even to me, was angelic, or that he had in fact never really seen me. Right then it was the setting sun just over my shoulder that set my compass, the otter having his dinner just out of my reach, the way even my face felt numb in the chill of that pre-summer twilight.

Day 18: Friday March 31, 1989

When we arrived at Sam and Kenya's Delaveaga home, I noticed things like ivy that climbed the entire façade of the two-storey, white house along redwood lattice; a tiny yellow light glowing out of general darkness in one of the upstairs bedrooms; the scent of bergamot coming from a little diffuser in the entryway; the stunning beauty of the mother of these two girls. Mrs. Hawthorne was friendly and kind, mildly interested in our evening but also happy to let us recede into the privacy of Kenya's bedroom. She carried in her hand a brandy snifter and wore a robe like a kimono the exact of her tourmaline eyes; that night they were blue.

"Goodnight girls," she said to us rather dreamily and then, "don't stay up too late." I watched as she lifted her glass to her forehead and slid her blond bangs off of her face with a pinkie finger before taking a sip and closing the door. When she had shuffled off to her own bedroom, Athena and Sam helped Jake in through the window, outside of which he had been clinging about twenty feet from the ground for at least three minutes.

He pretty much fell into the room in a little heap with Athena half underneath him, but he recovered quickly, laughing good-naturedly, if a little sheepishly, as he got to his feet.

"There's gotta' be an easier way!" he said as part of a long exhalation. He was picking dried ivy leaves off his shirt and allowing Athena to pull them tenderly out of his hair. Kenya was laughing at him softly and had already begun producing the accoutrements for mixed drinks from her backpack. We assembled ourselves in a loose circle, and I turned to Sam.

"So you guys are twins?"

"Yeah, fraternal," said Kenya, wielding a liter of Coke and a bottle of rum.

"Two eggs, two sperm. Ultra fertile parents," said Sam. Kenya scowled at the graphic nature of Sam's description of their engenderment, and perhaps at the unpleasant image it conjured, but she didn't protest. She was wearing a tie-dyed T-shirt and tiny round glasses with lenses the of summer sky. Her neck was adorned with several beaded chokers, and her face with a deep dimple on each side of her mouth. She extended a cup in my direction.

As if reading my mind, it was Athena who spoke: "You don't have to..."

"No," I said, "it's cool." I felt like an utter child and tried to be casual about taking the cup from Kenya.

"Whaaaaaat?" said Jake in disbelief. It was dawning on him in just how many ways I actually was a child.

"Owww!" he exclaimed when Athena whacked him in the chest with the back of her hand. I took an awkward sip and tried not to sputter, as my first inclination was to eject the contents of my mouth.

"You like?" said Kenya, raising her eyebrows, as if she hadn't even noticed my grimace.

"Yeah, it's not bad."

"That's okay. It's an acquired taste," said Sam, raising her cup in the air. "To new friends," she said, smiling a little wickedly, "and bad habits!"

We all toasted to this and murmured our agreement. Despite the churning already beginning in my stomach, there was nowhere I would rather have been right then. No one whose company I would have preferred to have.

"Questions?" suggested Athena mischievously.

"Not yet," said Kenya with significance.

"Why do you want to play at questions?" asked Sam.

"Why wouldn't she want to play at questions?" asked Jake mysteriously.

"Is there a game you'd prefer to play?" Sam said, turning to her sister.

"Do I ever play games?" asked Kenya, mock seriously. It was obviously a sort of game, and after a while I recognized it as the game of Questions from the Stoppard play, *Rosencrantz and Guildenstern are Dead*. My mom had had me read it as a companion piece to *Hamlet* when I was a sophomore. At the time its existential themes had left me in a fog of curious intrigue. These three had obviously read it, too.

"Not that kind of Questions! Come on, you guys!"

Athena was a little exasperated. Sam immediately pointed an imperial index finger at her.

"Foul, statement. Minus one for Athena."

"Is Athena not in a gaming mood?" patronized Jake playfully.

"What kind of mood is she in?" was Kenya's next question.

"Why does it have to be about my mood?" Athena's tone carried a hint of a whine.

"Is it about something else?" suggested Sam.

"Why are you always able to draw me in to this stupid game?" Athena continued to resist but managed to avoid racking up a negative score.

"Don't you like it?" teased Jake.

"Don't you like Jake?" Sam asked, shifting the mood instantaneously, though only momentarily. Jake became immediately interested.

"What?" he wanted to know. Athena shot Sam a warning look.

"Foul, non-sequitur," she proclaimed, "Minus one for Sam."

"Wait, what?!" asked Jake, now very interested but clearly powerless to stop the momentum of the game already ambling away from Sam's tiny revelation.

"Foul, repetition," said Kenya in her maternal tone. "Minus one for Jake."

"Who's making the rules in this game?" said Sam.

"Am I drunk?" I asked in a barely audible voice. Kenya smiled approvingly.

"Ha ha, she catches on quick!" she laughed.

"Foul, statement," said Jake quickly, pleased with himself. "Minus one for Kenya."

"Doesn't Kenya make all the rules?" Sam mused.

"Is there a rule about being a smart ass?" Kenya retorted.

"Wouldn't you know?" asked Jake, smirking.

"Doesn't that count as repetition?" Kenya asked in a high-pitched voice.

Meanwhile Athena, who had been flipping through a small book, asked her question: "Doesn't anyone want to answer a real question?"

"Are there any real questions?"

"Foul, rhetoric," said Sam gravely. "You're down by three, Jake." Jake shrugged and flopped onto his belly, Kenya's pillow wadded up under his ribcage.

"You know what I was thinking about today? Tonight, actually, while I was assuming the position, hanging off the lattice by my fingertips? Remember when we built that fort down by the stream at Athena's old house?"

"Yeah, and we stowed coins and almonds and fresh water in jars…" Athena began.

"In case of siege!" Kenya said, and they all laughed at the memory.

"Yeah! Sam had this whole 'kingdom' mapped out. What did she call it?" Jake asked.

"Anastasia!" Athena said. "Man, I'd forgotten about that."

"She went around with that little shovel trying to get rid of the mineral deposits on the banks, saying it was some infestation. What a little freak!" laughed Kenya, playfully teasing her 'little' sister.

Unfazed, Sam simply turned to me and said, "Jerks." Giggling, she lay back then on Kenya's tie-dyed beanbag. "I didn't hear any of you complaining about my vast imagination at the time, beneficiaries that you were! Oh, and Sidka was my prince!" she declared expansively, stretching her arms above her head and smiling in the reverie.

"My Siberian Husky," Athena said to me in explanation.

"He never wanted to wear his crown, though," added Sam, frowning. Jake, laughing, tossed a pillow that landed right on her face, and she pulled it off slowly, giggling again. She was feeling pretty good right about then, and I was still nursing my first drink.

It was Kenya's voice that drew my attention away from her purple lava lamp.

"Okay, first question," she said, taking the *Book of Questions* from Athena. "This one's for Jake."

"Why me?" he whined.

"Oh, c'mon you big baby," Sam said, nudging him with her knee. Kenya proceeded to the question, nonplussed, and read aloud.

"If you were able to wake up tomorrow in the body of someone else, would you do so? And if so, who would it be?"

"Uh, that's a no-brainer," said Jake, "Madonna."

"Pig," said Sam.

"God, Jake!" said Athena, annoyed. "He's not always like this," she said to me.

"Geez, lighten up, ladies! Okay, okay. Uh—Magic Johnson." Jake's amended answer seemed to satisfy the girls, and Athena took the book to continue the game.

Turning to me, she said, "Alright. Angela. An eccentric millionaire offers to donate a large sum to charity if you will step—completely naked—from a car onto a busy downtown street, walk four blocks, and climb back into the car. Knowing that there would be no danger of physical abuse, would you do it?"

"Depends on the charity," said Kenya, "Are we talking about whales or people?"

"In a heartbeat," said Jake coolly.

"It's Angela's question," chided Sam.

"Uh…I don't know, I…" I was trying so hard not to be lame. "I'm pretty shy about that stuff," I said.

"That stuff?" repeated Jake, still obviously alarmed by my naiveté.

"About my body," I explained, "but…if it's for charity." I thought I saw Jake roll his eyes then. Again, I paused and finally committed to my answer: "Yeah, I guess so."

"Good job," said Athena with a genuine smile. She handed me the book then, adding, "Your turn." I turned the pages slowly, reading the questions one after another. Many of them were intimate and required some sort of disclosure on the part of the answerer. I could see that Athena had been kind to me, had chosen a question that was fairly mild.

"Okay, Sam," I said, having found one I thought was particularly interesting. "If you were happily married, and then met someone you felt certain to always bring you deeply passionate, intoxicating love, would you leave your spouse?"

"So my spouse doesn't currently bring me deeply passionate, intoxicating love?" was Sam's question back to me, but it was Kenya who answered.

"Apparently not," she said flatly.

"Um. I don't know," Sam said.

"I think I'd just marry somebody who did bring me that kind of love," said Athena. I saw her glance shyly just then at Jake, who seemed slightly embarrassed, too. I wondered at their tentativeness with each other and considered the differences between a relationship in transition and one that is brand new...perhaps they were fewer than I had thought.

"Yeah, but...sometimes things change," said Sam.

"What if you had children?" I interrupted. It seemed to me like an important qualification to make.

"Then no way. I'd stay with the limpy spouse." Sam was unequivocal on this point.

"Really?" said Kenya, genuinely surprised.

"Yeah," said Jake, "kids are involved. Everything is different then." His conviction interested us all and we each turned to stare at him. Embarrassed, he added, less convincingly, "I think."

"Give me that," said Sam, taking the book from my hand. She took her time, trying to find a good question. When she looked at Athena mischievously, I thought I knew what she was up to, but she surprised me again.

"Do you believe in any sort of God?" she read. "If not, do you think you might still pray if you were in a life threatening situation?"

Athena was thoughtful, and I had already observed that she was usually careful with her words. She could be playful and silly, but when she was at ease, being serious, she seemed to weigh each syllable, arranging her words to convey her meaning.

"I believe in the Divine," she said. "In what's perfect. It can be in oneself, I think. Or outside of the self…still accessible somehow. It can be between two people, too, I think." Another glance at Jake. "Or among several." Then she was quiet.

"You've given this some thought," I said, rather in awe at the precision of her answer.

"Yeah. I guess I have. Though you just heard it all. That's pretty much the extent of what I think I know. It's a start, though."

"Yeah," I agreed, "a pretty good one."

We all fell asleep after a while, Kenya and Sam curled up on the bed, me in the beanbag, Athena and Jake on the floor with stuffed animals under their heads. I felt blissful as I drifted off, a little bit of a lilt to my stillness, from the rum. I was surrounded by friends. Yes. Surrounded by friends. They were too good, it seemed, but I abandoned caution, as only the young can, for the hope of myself someday becoming as bright as they appeared to me then.

I had a lucid dream that night. The most vivid one of my life:

I am in the trees outside of Kenya's window. I am moving around in the air, not flying exactly, but moving. I am not aware of my body as I know it, but of my self as light. I move effortlessly, quickly. Sam, Kenya and Athena are here, too, also weightless. I can't say we are without form. We are definitely something. We are our selves. Just without—limits. No sort of epidermis to contain what spills from us in what looks to me like little flourishes of fairy dust in our wakes. Jake is not here; I worry myself with trying to find him for a moment in the dream and then abandon the thought. Intuitively, I know I will not find him here. The other girls laugh and spar in the air, darting between trees, in and out of shadow. Moonlight falls on us like water, cool baptism of freedom. I feel I know the other girls intimately; we are like sisters.

It was the sound of rustling and whispers that woke me and drew my attention back to the windowsill, where the corporeal Athena and Jake were saying goodbye. Athena was leaning out, Jake hanging again from the lattice.

"Hey," she said as he began to descend.

"Yeah?" he asked.

"Write me a poem, okay?" she said tentatively.

"A poem?"

"Yeah. In your journal. Will you do it?" The expectation in her voice was palpable. I couldn't see him, but I heard his voice soften.

"Yeah. Sure." And then he was in the frame of the window again. Gorgeous in his goofiness. He kissed Athena quickly on the lips, paused momentarily to wonder at his own act and to rub his head where he had thumped it against the window frame. Suddenly he grinned and scrambled down the lattice.

"I'll see you Monday," I heard him call.

"See you Monday," I mouthed from the darkness beyond them, but it was Athena's voice that followed him into the night:

"Yeah, see you Monday."

When she turned around, she wore a distracted little smile. Then, pressing one hand against her mouth, she hugged herself with a tiny shiver. I pretended to sleep. She was so beautiful standing there in the window, encircled by moonlight, aglow in the newness of something that seemed always to have existed. I felt guilty at having let my voyeurism take such a tangible shape, but I couldn't let her know I had witnessed this momentous shift in her relationship with Jake. Couldn't let her see my own longing, not directed at anyone or anything in particular, but in this moment unleashed and with the power to reveal me.

Day 21: Monday April 3, 1989

Mrs. Girard, our quirky Italian art teacher with wild black curls that spilled over her shoulders and formed a veritable cloud around her head, was performing her rounds in her usual paint-splattered smock, today accented by rainbow-striped socks. She was walking slowly around the periphery of the circle formed by our easels. With our easels configured like this, she used to say, we are inspired by the presence of other artists, all within our view, but our creative impulses are not diverted or thwarted by seeing the work of those artists, all legitimate in their individual pursuits. I felt slightly less than legitimate in a class that had accommodated me primarily because I had already taken the equivalent of the requisite Painting I and Painting II courses and was by law prevented from taking them again for credit. I had no propensity for physical art, it seemed.

Athena was wearing the black smock that she always wore when she painted. It had belonged to her mother, and it had little scarlet pockets and a scalloped collar to match them. She was deep in thought, her paintbrush moving steadily over her canvas. When Mrs. Girard walked behind Athena, she stopped and sighed in a way that sounded to me like Yeeeeeesssss and Ooooooh. Then she sucked the air back into her lungs through the formidable gap between her front teeth and began the conversation we had heard her have with Athena on numerous occasions.

"Have you looked at the papers I gave you? On the

Rhode Island School of Design?"

"Yeah," said Athena dreamily, still deeply involved with her painting, which was taking the shape of a stylized infant adorned with varying shades of light. It appeared to be at the center of some gravitational pull, the source and attraction of so much and movement at once. I puzzled over this piece that seemed daily to grow out of blankness. I could see that she had named it "Birth."

"Some," Athena continued, "You know my dad has his heart set on USC for me. He was a Trojan, you know?"

"Yes. And you got your acceptance?" Mrs. Girard was dismissive whenever Athena mentioned her father and his wishes for a legacy at his Southern California alma mater. He had been a Communications major and had visions of his daughter on the ten o'clock news. Though she shared none of his aspirations to public recognition, Athena humoured her father and allowed herself to be guided by his hopes. Athena nodded absently in response to this last question, still absorbed in her work.

"And what is it that Athena Gates wants?" Mrs. Girard persisted.

Athena shrugged, giving Mrs. Girard none of the satisfaction she sought. "I don't know," she said. "It's hard to think that far ahead."

"Athena!" the elder woman shrieked, "Graduation is in less than two months!"

But she could see that there was no way to interest Athena in this particular discussion that day and perhaps out of respect for the creative process in which the beautiful girl was obviously engaged, she moved along to the easel of Alvin Ku. The unusually tall and ever reticent Korean exchange student was deeply absorbed in his own work and was unselfconsciously painting his self-appointed subject: Athena's profile.

It turned out Athena's dedication to the task at hand

was much more vulnerable than it had appeared at first, for when Jake poked his head in at the open door, composition book in hand, Athena immediately slipped off her painting smock and ducked out of the room, evading the gaze of our Italian taskmaster. Through the vertical windows of the building I could see them as they went, Jake laughing at Athena, who was hopping and leaping into the air in an attempt to reach the mottled black and white journal he held just out of her reach. The poem, I inferred, and as they moved finally beyond the last pane of glass that revealed them to me, I turned again to the strange and gritty-looking image that was taking shape on my own canvas.

When I saw Athena at lunch, being counseled by Sam, who was wearing her Walkman headphones around her neck and practically inhaling a cinnamon roll nearly the size of her head, I gathered that all had not gone well with Jake's poem. Licking white flakes of icing from her lips and moving things around absently to accommodate me, Sam gestured for me to sit near them. I took a seat on the bench and quietly unwrapped my vegan sandwich on rye bread, lovingly packed by my mother. Inwardly thrilled by Sam's invitation to lunch, I listened to their conversation, now and then contributing a carefully measured nod or a commiserating sigh.

"So he wrote you a poem?" said Sam, licking her fingers scrupulously. She leaned a hip against the picnic table, sipping chocolate milk with one of those tiny red straws meant for stirring coffee, oblivious to her beguiling effect on the boys in the vicinity.

"Yeah. But it was like—not for me. I mean..." I handed Sam the cloth serviette from my lunch bag, and she nodded her acknowledgement before wiping her mouth and proceeding.

"Not what you wanted," Sam said matter-of-factly.

"Well, it's not like I knew exactly what I wanted," said Athena, slightly defensive, "I just--"

"Wanted a love poem," said Sam.

"Would you stop doing that!" she cried, flustered.

"Well, am I right?" It was hard to be annoyed with Sam, even when she was this smug, and Athena smiled slightly.

"Yeah," she conceded.

"So tell him that." Things were always pretty black and white with Sam.

"Oh God," said Athena gravely.

"What, we've known him practically since we were born," Sam said casually, swinging her heavy backpack onto her shoulders. "He'll get it. He's crazy about you." Sam clearly did not consider this last admission to be new information, but Athena seemed slightly surprised.

"Really?" she asked.

"Oh brother," said Sam, "how do you not see that?" For Sam, the case was closed. She gathered up her lunch things and moved her headphones to her ears.

"Trust me," she said to Athena and, inconceivably, to the both of us: "We'll talk again tonight at Pip's, okay?"

Athena did not appear to be consoled, but I was gleeful at the prospect of joining them for their typical evening of cocoa and studying. It felt natural somehow, and I savored the sense of inclusion it gave me. Athena nodded her assent and I grinned foolishly as Sam made her way into the stream of students now moving toward their afternoon classes. When Athena looked back at me, I regained my sobriety, her sad little pout chiding me into seriousness. I held the last bit of my lunch out to her, as if in consolation, but she wasn't interested in a banana and refused it politely.

"You coming tonight then?" she asked me.

"Uh, yeah. Downtown, right?"

"Yeah. Cedar Street. Pip's is the big Victorian converted to a coffee house...the oldest one in Santa

Cruz. You can't miss it." She smiled widely and it occurred to me, not for the first time, how all three of these girls had the uncanny ability to make things right, in a single instant, under almost any circumstance. Just now Athena had slid the immediate discussion off easily, like she had her painting smock, and emerged with a voice like little bells, exuding such peacefulness, such ease. Yes, Athena's voice had bells in it. Not like Daisy Buchanan's bells in Fitzgerald's famous novel, but organic bells like wind chimes, like little musical whispers calling you ever back to the center of a moment. To the present.

"Cool," I said and left Athena beneath the maple tree where Jake had recited his poem a mere forty-five minutes earlier. He had left hastily, chafing against the seemingly apathetic reception of his ardent efforts in verse.

Pip's was ensconced by a wrap-around deck and surrounded by a variety of local shrubs and trees. The trees were strung through with hundreds of tiny white lights, and ever drifting from within were the clear notes of some ambient music, sometimes live but usually recorded. Always, there was some beatnik-looking fellow on the bench near the door, sipping on a cigarette and nodding to the gently animated gestures of a long-haired girl. Tonight she was blond and wore a crimson turtleneck with her miniskirt.

The downstairs rooms of the Victorian were all adorned with the work of the local artist of the month and were punctuated by square and round tables throughout, the coffee bar at its center. Kenya's favorite table was one near the bay window that had for seats what looked like church pews. It basked in the glow of a leaning Tiffany lamp that cast shades of purple and green. It was beneath this lamp that I found Kenya and Jake, who gestured for me to come join them. As I was unloading textbooks and highlighters, Athena and Sam also arrived.

"Hey, what took you guys so long?" said Kenya.

"Diving practice went long," Sam said. "Hey, Angela," she said to me, flicking my right ear softly. It was as if I had always occupied that place at the table. My casual greeting belied the excited little toss and flutter in my chest.

"Hi," I said.

"You should have seen her!" Athena said. "She did a perfect one and three quarters flip."

"One and three quarters?" Jake asked, standing to allow the girls to slide into the pew next to Kenya.

"Yeah, right onto her back," Athena said. "She landed perfectly flat. Didn't even sink."

"Ouch," said Kenya.

"Yeah, ouch," agreed Sam.

"Did you black out?" asked Kenya. Clearly this was not the first time Sam had experienced such a mishap at diving.

"No, not this time. But I barfed in the gutter."

"It was pretty gross," added Athena.

"You are as good as a chorus, m'lady," said Jake, bowing deeply to Athena and slightly altering Ophelia's line from *Hamlet*. I had learned that Jake's love of the play *Hamlet* was at the heart of many of his quips and quotes and had been the impetus for their game of Questions. Tonight he was testy; he had, after all, bared his heart to this bright angel, only to find her inexplicably displeased. He had tweaked Ophelia's tone, but the general drift matched.

In a moment, however, he had shifted his attention back to Sam, allowing the slight bitterness that had edged his voice to dissolve. "You're pretty hard core, Sam," he said, tousling her hair.

"Yeah, hard-core," I echoed almost inaudibly.

Jake was still on his feet and now offering to order the drinks. We all dug in backpacks and coin purses to come up with the buck fifty that it cost for a small cocoa. While he was gone there was a considerable amount of surreptitious talk about the tension that was obviously dictating Athena's interactions with Jake.

I thought then about how easy it is for us to tangle something so simple and fine as love, or even love's impetuous sister, infatuation. Athena and Jake so obviously adored one another. I thought to myself that any poem would have sufficed, had I been the subject and recipient of something penned by this wonderful boy. I had to admit to myself, too, though, that it would probably have been my wild and unyielding hope, as it had been Athena's, that the something penned might reveal, or at least hint at, romantic tendencies toward myself. Wasn't that the primary use of poetry?

Our study session went late into the night, and I knew my parents would be worried, so I began to pack up, but I wouldn't leave before venturing an invitation. With anyone else it would have been perhaps premature; it had been, after all, less than a month ago that I had truly met this group of friends. But something gave me the confidence to ask them.

"So, uh, it's your birthday next weekend, right?" I ventured, addressing all three girls. I had learned that the three of them shared a birthday and that their parents, who had been enrolled together in birthing classes at Dominican Hospital, had befriended each other before they were ever even parents. Athena's mother, who had not been due to give birth for another month, had expected to learn from Sam and Kenya's; instead she had ended up in labor in an adjacent room and hearing the wail of her own newborn within hours of the Hawthorne babies' first sputtering cries.

"April sixteenth. Not this Sunday but next," said Kenya.

"Mm—hmm," said Sam, and Athena explained again:

"I was supposed to be born a month later, but I was a preemie. We have this picture where the three of us are about three months old, and we're lined up in a row with like seven other babies on a big couch. I don't even know how they got us all propped up like that. It's such a funny picture!"

"Lamaze reunion," added Kenya. "You can barely see Athena's tiny little head poking out of her frilly little baby dress. She was so small!"

"She had so much hair she looked like a little monkey," laughed Sam.

"That's so cool," I said.

"We've had maybe two birthdays apart, yeah?" Sam asked the other girls.

"That year I was in Canada with my grandparents," Athena said.

"And the year Sam and I had the chicken pox," said Kenya. Turning toward Jake, she added, pinching his cheek affectionately: "And Jake's the baby. A whole year younger. Brainiac. Poet. You know the type."

I dove in then. Just asked them. My parents had a house at Lake Tulloch. It was a rustic but lovely little home right on the water with an enormous deck and a small, private dock for our ski boat. We had spent most of last summer lolling about on that deck and riding the wake of our boat at the end of a ski rope. Tonight, I felt intrepid. I felt ready to give, ready to receive, in a way I never had. I could invite these four up to our lake house for the day on Sunday, and we could celebrate the three birthdays together. That night, we could drive back together in Kenya's van, leaving my parents alone in the Landcruiser to pull the boat home.

"We could water ski and stuff," was the brilliant lure I cast into the water. I could really disappoint myself verbally sometimes.

"Yeah," said Sam, enthusiastically, "We're celebrating with family on Saturday anyway. And Kenya can drive the van!"

"Will it make it?" asked Jake, eternally teasing Kenya about her VW bus.

"Hey!" she said, pretending to be deeply offended and then settling back in her seat, arms crossed over her chest. "Flower power, dude. Not a problem," she added ridiculously.

And just like that, it was happening. I felt irrationally validated; here were four pretty exceptional human beings who wanted to hang out with me. And with them, I was who I was. I didn't feel I had to appear a certain way or hide what was in my heart (with the exception of the errant fondness for Jake that sometimes swelled there).

The next two weeks were full of anticipation and that night, after the coffee house, fretted with fleeting thoughts of what we would eat, what we would do, how I would introduce them to my parents. For now I felt at ease. I felt happily excited. I believed in something lovely.

I surfed almost every day those next two weeks. I left campus straight away each afternoon and zoomed up to the cool and quiet refuge of Davenport, where I could dive into the ocean and keep company with harbor seals and the occasional dolphin. I felt my way through evenings wrapped in sea kelp, sunsets swirling above the gently swelling sea.

I savored moments with my new friends at school, talked to Sam or Athena on the phone occasionally and dreamed of a perfect weekend at the lake, all of us moving under a sun just gathering its summer heat. The plans were in place, and I felt myself growing into the more social, less self-conscious girl I would become in time. I was in no way ready to allow this girl to be seen by anyone else, not ready to reveal her in my dress, in my gestures or words, but I sensed her in myself, and I felt instinctively that these girls, they sensed her too.

Three

Angela

I don't know exactly what passed between Athena and Jake that night after Pip's. There were many strained exchanges during our little study session, both verbal and nonverbal. There were furtive glances one at the other, and there was a deep sadness that such a rift could have made its way into their friendship. This, above all, pervaded the mood of all of us at the table. The ice between them was just beginning to melt when Kenya, Sam and I finally called it a night, packing away our study materials and yawning overtly. Jake and Athena looked slightly uncomfortable but ready to have a moment alone.

I think that once we'd gone, the two of them must have walked into the spring night together. They must have moved among the giant elms that line the streets in that part of town, bundled against the coastal chill with Athena's violet scarf, Jake's black beanie. Athena must have admitted her desire for a 'love poem,' and Jake must have melted in the realization of all that this secret desire denoted. He would have forgiven her immediately the humiliation of her unfavorable reception of his offered language. He would have loved her the more for being shy to tell him. For her tentativeness. For her vulnerability.

I think he must have taken her into his arms and let his mouth linger on her forehead, on both of her eyes, her lips. What I know he did not do, and this would become a source of significant torment to him in the months to come, was take her to his bed. They were young, and Jake carried the most profound respect for Athena. Never would it have occurred to him to ask this of her so soon.

Whatever that night looked like, whatever words were exchanged, whatever touch indulged, the two of them were transformed. The following two weeks were for them a blissful consummation of what had been growing between them since before they could ever have been aware of such seeds. They were inseparable and while they did not alienate me or the others, something told us to respect this bubble of time. It was a protracted moment of discovery, the clues for which had littered the path leading to these surreal days between life one way and life another.

Life indeed, for what is death but change? The transformation from existence on one plane to existence on the next. The releasing of one's "mortal coil" and the embracing of all that is light and perfect and divine in the self. The part that is without limitation. Without flesh and bone. Without an angel you knew was your own.

Four

Angela

When I woke in the hospital, I felt heavy, as if I had absorbed all the water of the lake. I felt bloated with my dread. It took only moments for me to leap from that groggy state of semi-consciousness to the sharpness of panic. The faces of my parents warned me not to ask the question, not to seek the words that would break me.

"It's not your fault," was the mantra that kept being repeated by almost everyone who came to my bedside. It was like an absurd parade of mourners, and I was immobilized in a sterile room under a sterile blanket, a sterile apology rising from an unknown place in my consciousness. Mercifully, sleep overtook me at regular intervals, and I could leave those faces and their uniform assurances in the realm of the conscious. The realm of the real.

I don't remember any of my dreams with any clarity, but I know my mind ran them without ceasing, for all the hours I slept in that hospital bed. I remember them like I remember most things, in that impressionistic way my mind reconstitutes the past. Without being able to name their content, I can say that embedded within those dreams were images from every aspect of my short time with Jake, Athena, Sam and Kenya. There were their faces. Their voices. Whispers and screams. Things turning themselves inside out and righting themselves again. Oil and acrylic, canvas shrouds, spinning wheels of and light. Silent crashes re-enacted in bits and pieces left me cold and panting as I woke alone, with only the glow of monitors to light my waking way and guide me again into that restless sleep.

Of course I was never actually alone. My mother slept in the chair near my bed for three days straight, knowing I would heal but fearing my regret upon waking, truly waking, from the ordeal. Fearing my loss and the moment I would fully register it. She was clinging to the evidence that she had *not* lost in the way the Hawthorne and the Gates families had. She clung to my inaudible breath and the gentle rise and fall of my chest in spite of four broken ribs. Irrationally, for my wounds were never fatal, she imagined my sudden expiration at intervals, like she had when she had been a new mother and I, in my infant stubbornness, had preferred to sleep on my belly. Those moments had taken years off her life, she used to declare, laughing, whenever she recounted her vigilance over her sleeping baby—alas the only one to whom she would give birth. The one who would become a late blooming teenager. The one whose fault it definitely was not.

I was good at accepting my innocence. Better, I think, than your average teenager would be. I seemed to have an innate sense of the transience of life, of its absurdity, and this last, most absurd of occurrences, served to reinforce my lack of faith in the universe to provide meaning. Being at the wheel did not equal my guilt; I knew that. My intellect colluded with this formula. There was no way, the marina officers would assure me later, alluding to forensics studies and the science of speed, that I could have anticipated the crash. No way for me to have avoided such a collision. And miraculously, I had not yet cracked a beer for myself, which lifted the potential for questions around that kind of culpability. It was a freak accident. One where the actions of individuals aligned for several consecutive moments in a way that resulted, as if by design, in a fantastic explosion of matter and of life.

When life began to come into focus again, for me, there did not have to be meaning attached to the incident; my initial numbness enabled such indifference. I had doubted the legitimacy of expecting life to provide meaning for some time, and though these girls had lured me toward a more romantic, less existential approach, their deaths left me right back where I started—except without the question of God. For how could a loving God allow such waste of life? Such suffering of his subjects. How could a benevolent God bestow such a gift and then yank it away so precipitously? No, this settled that matter for me, and I was determined, finally, that I was alone in the world. Nietzsche's character was right when he said, "God is dead," I reflected, willing to concede that God might have lived at one point. Absurd experience had shown me that he lived no longer.

Jake's distance from me supported this belief, as well, for the cruelty of his silence, though benign enough, left me broken-hearted. He was clearly not willing to admit my suffering, so diminutive was it compared with his own. But I have learned since then, that there are not degrees of suffering. Only different lenses through which to see it. In those days I imagined myself as foreign to the whole scene, alone and absurd myself, in an absurd enactment of human suffering.

Like every other detail, the timing puzzled me. That I should have enjoyed such a short time with these three whose lives and love had left such an impression on me. I knew my grief to be lesser in degree than, say, that of their parents or their siblings. Certainly less than that of Jake, who seemed to want to keep this distinction at the fore, always. But it was real grief. Real loss.

Once, much later in my life, I attended the funeral of a boy who had died in an avalanche. Josh was the son of a friend of mine and I had known him well when he was a young boy but then lost my sense of him as he had grown apart from his parents and moved to a boarding school in the Swiss Alps. I flew with Margaret to Switzerland to see him ed by his teachers and peers there. At the memorial, I was struck by the intensity of the grieving housekeepers, all Serbian women, for there was a confluence of eastern European families living in this small Swiss town, all working in maintenance or housekeeping jobs for the American school there.

I remember thinking that they must barely have known Josh, these women who cleaned his private dormitory bathroom, who probably swept his floor and emptied his trash can every week. And yet, how real their grief. By that time in my life, this observation was quick to find its place in my conception of the scene: it was the grief of mothers for sons. Period. It was more primal than empathy, perhaps more primal even than a sense of injustice. It was simply how a woman recognizes the unnatural and tragic confusion around seeing one's own child die. Of course if you compared their grief with that of Margaret, it seemed exaggerated, obscene even. But of itself, it was a legitimate response to the death of a boy.

We go through life and we go through life and then one day—this. The death of a child. The repercussions of that, the thousand immeasurable aftershocks, large and small, who can judge? It raises the first question. It raised the first question for me, I should say, and every question has risen out of that first one ever since. Zora Neale Hurston said, "Some years ask questions, some years answer them." I think every year does both; only sometimes it is the question that resonates. Sometimes the answer.

Looking back now, the events of my life sliding together in their fluid palette, I become indistinguishable from Svetlana, the Serbian housekeeper's daughter I met on that trip to Switzerland for Josh's funeral.

Svetlana had cleaned Josh's bedroom with her mother during the two weeks of her winter break from Swiss school. Once, she had discovered a note to his girlfriend and pretended it was written to herself. She didn't know what Josh looked like; there was no photo to show her the face of the boy she had imagined up. The proprietor of size eleven ski boots and a miniature Eiffel Tower. When he disappeared she was crushed with him, as under the three meters of snow that buried his body at the bottom of the chute. She cried for days and was judged a fool by her peers, who also did not know the boy.

Accompanying Margaret, my broken friend, to the burial of her boy, I held that Serbian girl's head against my chest, while her mother wept with the other housekeepers. My baby French made the most tenuous bridge between us:

"Pleure, ma cherie. C'est triste." *Cry, my darling. It's sad.* But there was no less truth in those words than there might have been in a more verbose commiseration in perfect English or Serbian. It was terribly sad. That is all.

For Jake, admitting *my* loss—or even the heaviness of having been behind the wheel— during that time would have been to mitigate his own grief, and child that he was, he hadn't the strength. I suspect he judged me weak, dramatic, foolish even.

My parents, my connection to whom seemed irreparably severed by the trauma of the collision, could not reach me. Those moments in darkness on the lake, gasping for air among the flaming remnants of two boats, Jake's voice calling Athena's name from somewhere across the undulant space between us, left me far out at sea, alive but only just. Alive but longing for sleep and solitude.

I was gone from them, like Sam, Athena and Kenya were gone from their families, but unlike them, I had the benefit of still inhabiting a body, still moving and breathing in my limbo between living and dying. With the benefit of time, I would heal and come back to them; I would heal and slowly allow myself to be reeled back in like an iridescent fish, my body set gently down on the hot sand. Sam, Athena and Kenya—they were not coming back.

The memorial service was held in the Chapel of the Four Seasons on Cayuga Street. It was a very rustic redwood building filled from floor to ceiling with wild-looking greenery growing out of planters built into the polished cement floor. The effect was that of a very large greenhouse, the light coming into the space at angles and in gentle shades of , compliments of stained glass high up in the A-framed walls. It has always stood out to me as the most peaceful place on earth…and, paradoxically, the one filled with the greatest longing. Longing for three beautiful spirits gone so soon as to have left an entire community of people without their bearings and trying to catch their breath. It is always so when young people die. This I have learned. But here were three, taken in an instant. The impact was devastating.

The service was for all of them together, life-sized portraits of each girl set among white floral arrangements at the front of the chapel. I remember feeling as if I were on a ship, traveling through my own *heart of darkness,* there in that sunlit glade of trees and plants that confused the mind, set it somewhere out of doors, away from the present situation—among the *wild things,* perhaps, but away.

The soft music of a lone harp kept drawing me back. That and the gentle moans of Athena's mother, Mrs. Gates. She, too, had black hair, though hers was shot through with fine streaks of white, and like Athena, she had a kind of numinous quality in her eyes. Now she crumpled against her husband, who held himself erect, an absurd flagpole to her limp and lifeless flag. Athena's five-year-old sister Camille drew tiny pictures of horses in a Hello Kitty diary at her father's other side, carefully separating herself from what she instinctively knew as too heavy to bear.

Once I heard her humming a little tune, some nursery rhyme or other, but her mother's thin hand on her knee was understood as the signal to stop, and Camille became quiet again; I watched her tear a tiny page out of her book, fold it neatly four or five different ways, and push it down into the little pocket at the center of her chest. She wore a burgundy jumper with a pink blouse underneath, stylized pink tulips adorning the pockets and hem.

Funny what you remember. I couldn't have told you what anyone else was wearing, but Camille's jumper, her pink tights and black patent leather shoes are engraved on my mind's eye. Perhaps it was hearing the story how, later that week, Mrs. Gates had collapsed in a heap of socks and T-shirts when, upon doing laundry, she had found the folded paper in the pocket of the little jumper, Athena's name scrawled in a five-year-old's hand across the page.

Mrs. Hawthorne wore enormous sunglasses in the fashion of Jackie Onassis. She clutched a white handkerchief to her chest when she was not pressing it rhythmically to her forehead, as if she were enduring great heat, though the chapel was cool to the point of chilliness. She kept a strained distance from her husband on the pew, her chin lifted slightly, as if to balance a book on the top of her head. Mr. Hawthorne, whom I had met only once, looked stricken, like a strange and volatile animal, an expression of near panic frozen on his suntanned features. Always during the ceremony, it seemed as if he would speak, but he did not.

At one point a young woman, twenty or so, took the

floor and sang, with a crackling track playing in the background, Alphaville's "Forever Young." This sprang a new well of tears, particularly among the youth assembled, and I remember feeling angry, manipulated somehow. As if our own sensations were not enough, here was someone's tragic cousin to send her bone-shaking alto above our heads to deliver lyrics that on any spring afternoon might evoke tears. But on this spring afternoon—through a saltwater blur—I took note of shuddering shoulders in a sea of muted s, as people of all ages sobbed silently, indulged personal griefs at which no one else could guess.

And then there was Jake. Jake was introduced as Athena's boyfriend by the frail-looking priest with owl-eyes and a thin comb-over. The Gates family had requested that he read a poem today.

I had heard the mothers, all four of them outside my hospital door, speaking of the night Jake had read this poem, again and again, into Athena's ear where she lay in the critical care unit. Bloated and pale, still with splinters of fiberglass in her hair, she had lain there in the moments before it was determined that no amount of electricity was going to animate her again. Her grandmother had rocked in silence not two feet away, but Jake had behaved as if he were alone with Athena, as if she could hear and would soon wake to acknowledge his longing. To thank him again for the poem that was not quite right but was the most perfect expression of his love thus far. *How* he must have wished for another week, a few days even, to craft the love poem she had wished for in her heart.

He had read the poem with his lips brushing her ear, her cool cheek touching his own. He had lit a candle to keep a vigil for the only one of the three girls who had survived this long, and kept it lit until she finally expired. It was a choice, and her parents made it with grace. They had allowed Jake as much time as he desired with Athena, whose lungs rose and fell not of her own accord now but in rhythm with a pump beside her bed. He had whispered again and again into her ear, "Bye Athena, bye Athena, bye Athena," weeping privately for everything they had not yet done, everything they had not yet said.

His grief was pure. Innocent. His love was real. These moments, though he barely knew to reflect on them at the time, would slowly leech away his faith; slowly leave him husk-like and full of an impossible dream that to everyone else looked like thin air.

At the service, he wore a black suit and tie, stood with his arm in a sling; oddly, the only injury he had sustained in the accident was a broken shoulder. I'm sure it did not help him to have emerged almost completely unscathed from the event that ended such a vast part of his life—that which *was* Athena, Sam and Kenya. That which held his deepest love.

When he opened his mouth to speak, nothing came out at first. Each syllable thereafter seemed wrenched from somewhere deep in his gut. "I," he began. Then nothing.

"I wrote this for Athena. I wasn't even sure what it was about when I wrote it. I'm not even sure I understand that still." His voice was shaky but his gaze was steady. He met my eyes once but showed no sign of recognition. Trance-like, he continued.

"She didn't like it very much at first. She—she wanted a love poem. In a way, it is. It's like I wrote it for myself. For today."

Again that sense of voyeurism rose in my heart. I almost didn't want to hear the poem. Absurdly, I felt like I was imposing…just by being part of the audience to which he spoke and now shared the poem that, in my mind, had grown to mythic proportions. Jake cleared his throat and hardly read the poem, for it was committed to his memory.

"Okay. Here goes:

I know and you know
I can see through the window.
I went this way you said before,
it is you whom I adore.
Picture perfect,
comfortably numb,
do your homework until sun.
I see deep into your eyes,
we have no time to criticize.
Jump the magic, it's up to you.
Hurry up, the sky is blue."

When he was finished, he paused awkwardly, looking to the priest and then adding, almost as an afterthought, "I loved her." He said this to Mrs. Gates, who seemed barely cognizant of his attention on her. He seemed to be pleading with her somehow, though she was no longer in the Chapel of the Four Seasons but floating above it somewhere, searching for her child, while her body shrank from this moment in the arms of her husband. Then Jake collected himself, closed his composition book and took his seat.

Five

Jake

"I went this way, you said before. " I pored over my own poem then, as if it held the code for understanding what had just happened in my life. The words seemed foreign, as if written by a stranger, but full of meaning. The only meaning I cared about in those days. "We have no time to criticize," as if I had known on some level what was to come. But then I would reject such blind belief in mystical happenings, understand the words as a fatalistic expression of the trite admonition to "live each day as if it's your last." Nothing new, nothing foreshadowing. Though I wanted to believe that Athena existed somewhere now, beyond the realm of the living, I could not fit the events of the past two weeks into my Christian conception of life and death, heaven and hell. No God of mine could have allowed this to happen. No God of mine was heartless enough to sacrifice such wonderful creatures for the sake of a test or a lesson. And how could I be so egocentric as to consider their deaths as a personal test for me? Hadn't I been always bound to fail such a test? I who was hopelessly in love, even now? It felt like a set-up.

I was a mess, and seeing Angela there in the chapel, I knew I should go to her, should acknowledge the importance of our shared experience, but I could not. This, I think, I will always regret. Though her grief was different from mine, it was real. And she carried around the burden of culpability. There was a moment, as everyone was filing out, when she paused with her eyes on me, asking the question of forgiveness. I remember the light coming in through the high stained glass windows, how it fell on her hair, lit her like some ethereal creature for a moment; then she shifted her weight on her feet, moved into shadow again, her eyes blinking behind the lenses of her glasses.

That day at the Chapel of the Four Seasons, I walked away from Angela, allowed myself to be absorbed by another circle of people who wanted to commiserate. After that, she was gone.

I didn't see her at the Gates' house, where many of us gathered to continue to tell stories about Kenya, Sam and Athena. There was a great deal of food, which filled the house with a sickly sweet kind of smell, and there were small children in their Sunday best, running and playing on the lawn in the back yard. I stood in the doorway of the little room where family and friends were gathered to watch a video of me, Sam, Kenya, and Athena enacting our seventh grade drama project, which featured me in tights and Athena in a clown suit.

Mrs. Gates approached me then; her attention toward me functioned as a kind of salve. Acknowledgement from her, whose grief was by far the most significant of anyone in my estimation, was the benediction I sought. Small irony that it was precisely that benediction of which I myself deprived Angela.

"Come with me, Jake," she said softly, gently ushering me by my elbow up the stairs to Athena's art loft. I had been in it many times, though in the past six months she had grown slightly secretive and had not invited me up. I had not taken it personally or as any kind of sign but respected her privacy, knowing I could admire her as easily from the ground level. My affection for her had grown exponentially over the past year, and I hardly knew how to behave anymore. Though I had known her since I became conscious of knowing, the feelings she stirred in me that year were new: a strange alchemy of the kind of admiration felt by a younger brother, which had constituted the greater part of my sentiment toward her since I had been a small boy trailing after the 'big girls' and hanging on their every word, and the confusing arousal I secretly felt for characters like Ophelia, Portia, and even Desdemona as I read them into life.

I considered it tragic that I had not recognized that Athena harbored similar feelings for me until the last few weeks of her life, and I told God that in anger, in the days I still spoke to him. Told him I resented recognizing the Shakespearean elements of misunderstanding, regret, tragic response, darkness and death in my own experience and then, paradoxically, fed myself on the drama it exuded.

In the loft, there were three easels, each draped over with a paint-splattered scrap of drop cloth. The walls were decorated in every manner of shape and , highlighting images of the feminine divine, which seemed to interest Athena more and more in the days before her death. Kuan Yin held out her clay vessel, meant for collecting tears; Mother Mary bent her head over the Christ-child in painting after painting by Rafaello, Leonardo, Mancini, all clipped from a calendar Athena had bought on a trip to Rome with her family. It was years later that I saw any connection in Angela's graduation gift to me, a tiny brass figurine of the goddess Tara. But that would come later.

In the art loft, I tried to ignore the pair of knee high Doc Marten's, kicked off haphazardly some afternoon before the lake trip, perhaps before Athena flopped into her papasan chair to the crooning sounds of Fugazi in the background. Methodically and slowly, Mrs. Gates removed the drape from each of the paintings to reveal a row of private works Athena must have done very recently.

The first was a painting of me, full of and movement, that seemed to capture my goofiest expression—painted from no photograph of which I was aware, but from Athena's infallible memory. In it I seemed to lunge forward, sending my silent laughter into the room beyond the canvas. The resemblance was uncanny. I was wearing her favorite T-shirt, my Social Distortion concert tee, and my hair was in wild disarray. I looked incredibly happy.

The second was a painting that looked eerily like Athena, though the female figure in it was oddly out of focus. She wore a kind of tulle skirt that fell in full folds toward the floor, her Doc Martens just visible beneath it. She wore a camisole, her bare shoulders angular and brown, as I remembered them. She appeared to be walking away from any viewer, at this moment from me and Mrs. Gates, her head turned over her shoulder to watch us as she went; her left hand trailed behind her in an almost-wave, and what looked like yellow light, or even glitter, emanated from her fingertips. The word "Departure" was scrawled in the bottom corner of the canvas, her signature beneath it in her loopy script.

The third painting was the image of a hand. It was much less realistic, but one could make out a wrist, fingers, even nail beds among the whirling s and shapes that suggested very fast movement around it. It was hard to tell if the hand was emerging from such chaos…or entering it. The painting was called "Passage."

Mrs. Gates looked mildly troubled. "Had you seen any of these before?"

"No," I said, shrugging and shaking my head.

"You didn't know she was doing your portrait?" she asked almost suspiciously. I shook my head.

"Or her own?" she added with raised eyebrows.

"No," I said again, thinking it useless to suggest that the girl in the second painting might be someone other than Athena.

Mrs. Gates held my gaze for a short time, tears beginning to fill her shadowy eyes. She shook her head and shoulders almost imperceptibly, as if to shiver away a thought, and began to remove the painting of me from the easel. I watched as she lifted it gently away, laid it on the futon and began to roll it up carefully. Then, hesitating for a moment, she rose again to take the painting of Athena from its easel, too, and laid it gently on top of mine. She rolled them together, slowly and deliberately, without speaking. From among the items lying on a small table against the wall, she fished a lavender ribbon I had seen Athena wear around her neck on many occasions, sometimes with a small black ornament hanging from it, nesting in the hollow between her collarbones. Mrs. Gates looped the ribbon around the rolled canvases and extended the bundle toward me.

"I wanted you to have your portrait. Did you see the title?" she asked. I shook my head again, and she paused, carefully pulling back the corner of the painting to reveal Athena's name and above it, simply, the word "love." My heart seemed to dry up again, to disintegrate, its essence stinging the insides of my ribcage as it spread there, like ash. Mrs. Gates was remarkably composed; she smoothed the corner back into place and put the bundle into my arms. Her tears were gone when she spoke again, her voice tinged with weariness.

"The other I can't bear to look at," she said. I thanked her and took my leave. She was still in the art loft, maybe even still on the lime-ed futon, when I opened the front door of the Gates' house to go.

I lived a short walk from there in a house overlooking the yacht harbor. It was the beach home of my mother's boyfriend. She lived there in wait for him to make his Santa Cruz rounds and grace us with his presence for a week or two at a time. He was a musician, ten years younger than she, and even I saw how ludicrous was my mother's idea that she was his 'partner'; but I kept quiet and ate from his china, sailed his Laser II and bathed myself in his granite-tiled shower. My mom drove his convertible Jaguar around town, talking on his car phone and pretending to be someone's wife.

Instead of going home I walked down onto the sand at the river mouth. Uncharacteristically large waves battered the jack-shaped stones of the jetty to the south, the light tower getting doused by seawater with every relentless set of waves. The weather was stormy for April. April twenty-third. Seven days after their birthday. The day of their death. I lay down then, paying no attention to the sand in my hair, filling my pockets, my shoes.

I felt numb and very small lying there, the swollen moon pale but already visible in the early evening sky. I felt tired, as if my entire belief system had been shot out of a cannon and left me to languish. This was how I would come to express it. Nothing I had believed, or thought I knew, existed as it had before that day. Without my full understanding, that crash, that loss, became the compass that set my course for the many years to come. April sixteenth was the day *I* was shot from a cannon, and I didn't have the heart to begin looking for the pieces of self I knew must be out there somewhere.

Six

Angela

I didn't go back to school. Perhaps I should have. It's hard to know what might have evolved. It could have been that the other students would have embraced me, would have shown me in their various ways that they knew I was not to blame. But I had never experienced them as compassionate beings and didn't imagine them capable of such kindness as I needed then. I did not believe that any event, tragic or otherwise, could precipitate such a change in people whom I had witnessed behave so carelessly toward one another and so exclusively toward me. Plus, with the exception of what was now irretrievable, I had failed to develop any meaningful friendships with any of them, including Jake. In my cynicism, I negated the opportunity to let them help me heal.

My parents were too weary to oppose my wishes, and they kept me home, nursing their own need to coddle me, protect me from the world into which I must inevitably return. I had miraculously escaped the fate of my friends, and these felt to them like stolen moments. It was like a surprise and bittersweet redemption: a free month of inseparability from their little girl who might have died and who would certainly otherwise have been making the final movements in her claim of independence and autonomy.

Instead of going shopping for prom dresses and signing yearbooks, I was immersed in water. Where I could not bring myself to ask for such acceptance from other people, I could give myself wholly to the ocean. It was water that had changed my life so unfathomably, and it was water into which I retreated for solace and much needed silence.

I plunged headlong into enormous waves, punching through to their hulking backs, only to spin on my board's tail and paddle onto faces that received me, propelled me forward, sometimes punished me gently and spit me out. Again and again I surfed, my mother's frail figure huddled on the beach, gazing seaward, her hands clasped in what appeared to me a continuous prayer. What went through her mind during those days, I will never know for sure, but I spared her fearful heart nothing in the risks I took in that ocean. Somehow I lived through one of the biggest spring swells ever to hit our coast, my mother and father silently enduring my recklessness for fear of pushing me away again.

As for Jake, what I felt before as a crush had become beyond complex and confused me to the point of tears. My desire to comfort the boy who had shared this experience with me was overwhelming, but that desire was countered by knowing that he considered me at least partly responsible for his grief. While it wasn't my fault (I was so tired of hearing that), didn't my actions that night form a critical part of the chain of events that became, ultimately, his incredible loss? I writhed under the knowledge that while he grieved, there was nothing that I could do to alleviate what tormented him; in fact, he would probably have refused me had I tried.

Ultimately, I decided to go to graduation, but by then I felt myself as a painted figurine, bustled and bobbing along in a current of bodies and sounds, separate from everything and everyone that surrounded me. I was beginning to heal myself, to accept things as they are, and even to soften toward other people, but this scene of ceremony and celebration only served to alienate me further. When it was over, I had only to find Jake and give him my gift, which I knew he would not understand but which had meaning for me, and it was such meaning that I clung to in those days.

I saw myself as infinitely capable of healing Jake, helping him, but by circumstance tragically prevented from doing so. Perhaps it was the perceived limitlessness of naïve youth, but looking back, I think there existed in me the dormant seeds of a very real kind of love. It was this that gave me the intrepidity to offer up my gift to him, this which provided the lens through which I viewed our relationship to one another, tenuous as our link was at the time.

Seven

Jake

Angela and her parents decided that she would not return to school after that. There were only a few weeks until graduation, and I think it seemed easier to them to finish it out home schooling, sheltered from the questioning gazes of our peers and the daunting task of facing those who might blame.

At graduation, I still wore a sling, and a long, thin wound still shone on Angela's forehead, though it would disappear in time. Our presence seemed to remind everyone of the diminished joy of the occasion, and I imagined their mild resentment toward us for robbing them of some of that beauty to which everyone feels entitled. I felt strange and out of sorts. After the ceremony, in my long black robe, I wandered the parking lot aimlessly, keeping an eye out for my mother who had gone to the car to "freshen up." Somehow Angela found me. She had a small white box in her hand, and a card.

"Jake," she called tentatively. She seemed smaller than she had before, more vulnerable. Her date-ed hair fell in waves around her shoulders, and she had an expression on her face that I could not identify. We had not really spoken since the accident. I had paid my obligatory visit in the hospital, under the watchful eyes of her parents, asked her how she felt, when she would get out, completely avoiding the subject of our dead friends. Such is the ineptitude of a young boy to deal with something so large, so impressive as death. I avoided her thereafter, not processing my inability to face her and uninterested in making sense of my unkindness. She might have held a grudge against me for my behavior in those first few days, those first few months. But she did not.

I slowed down enough for Angela to catch up to me. "Hey," she said softly.

"Hey." We sat down under a maple tree near the tennis courts, my mother nowhere to be seen in her red car. Timidly Angela extended the little box toward me, gesturing for me to take it.

"Oh, I…I didn't," I stammered, not having a gift to reciprocate. She simply smiled, clearly eager for me to receive hers.

"Open it," she said. I did. It was a small brass figurine of the Hindu deity Tara.

"It's Tara," she explained. "The goddess of feminine compassion."

"It's nice," I said stupidly, turning it around in my hand, but something occurred to me just then, and I became aware of the heft of this little figure in my hand. Someone had made this. Probably somewhere in Indonesia. I lifted it up and down, surveying it, weighing it with my consciousness. Angela looked a little puzzled but sat patiently, waiting for me to finish.

"This is real," I said aloud. I didn't even know exactly what I meant by it, but it rang true in my own ears. Here was something there need be no questions about. It was a symbol, on more levels than one, but it was a thing, a *real* thing, and *that* meant something. I spoke impulsively:

"I've decided I'm not going to waste my time on

anything that's not *real* anymore. This is real. In my hand. From you," I said and added, "Thank you." I knew I was making only a tenuous kind of sense, at best, but Angela was unfazed. She did not ask me to explain myself, didn't question my faltering; it was her way, I was learning. And now, as I was emphatically declaring a rather clumsy and amorphous resolution with unearned authority, she looked at me wide-eyed and without judgment. Instead she told me the story of Tara.

"It is said that she sprang from the tears of the bodhisattva, who was working so hard and felt so discouraged that he began to weep. She emerged from his tears—to help him in his work. To keep him strong."

I nodded, understanding her. Somehow, Angela knew the work that I was doing, saw the agonizing task in which I was engaged. It was the work of trying to believe something, of trying to reconcile myself to the way my life had changed. Life had been one way, and now it was another. I found this new way unbearable, and I saw no way out but to muddle through the fragments of my belief system, trying to piece it together in a way that might form a whole picture. It didn't occur to me then that she was engaged in the same struggle. That she, too, was sorting through the bits of her faith that might remain, searching out the stories, songs and myths that might replace what was irretrievably lost that night at the lake. And it certainly did not occur to me that she, Angela, was offering herself to me. My personal Tara.

"I'll be gone all summer," she said hesitantly, "but I'll see you in the fall." I knew that she was leaving with her parents who were shooting an entire Patagonia catalogue in Peru. She would probably spend the summer surfing and reading books, completely alone.

"Go Mustangs," she said defeatedly, a small fist in the air, a crooked smile on her lips. We were to attend the same university; by chance our paths were further entwined.

"Yeah, I'll see you," I said absently, still looking at the figure in my hand. Angela looked over my shoulder and gave a broad smile to my mother, who was just pulling up in the Jaguar.

"Hello, Mrs. Jameson," she said. My mom was holding the car phone to her ear. Its black spiraling cord lay between her augmented breasts, embarrassingly outlined by a red wraparound dress.

"Hello, Angela," she said sweetly through matching lips. "You ready, Jake?"

"Yeah," I answered, distracted. "I've gotta' go," I said to Angela, getting up and walking toward the passenger side of the car. Angela slid the envelope she had carried into my hand as I passed. I took it absently.

"See you," I said over my mother's head and, "Thanks, Angela."

Angela smiled weakly and waved, as I popped open the glove box and stuffed the card inside. As we drove away, I thought I saw Angela crying, but instead of processing this, I turned on the radio, letting my senses be assaulted by the Violent Femmes, a too bright sun, and the passing awareness that my youth was behind me now. Gone.

PART TWO

Spring 1995

Eight

Jake

I have journals and journals full of what could aesthetically be considered garbage. When one is truly suffering, suffering to such an extreme, that is all that comes. I wanted to die in the weeks and months following the accident. I had the irrational idea that the girls waited for me somewhere just beyond my consciousness. I think I believed that if I could just open myself into my dreams or transcend conscious thought for a minute or two, I might be visited by those who had possessed my heart for so many years, might have one more chance at feeling Athena near me, her soft breath on my neck or in my hair. I imagined that they filled the air around my ears, swirled there in their delicious freedom from flesh, just beyond the scope of my senses.

Over time my intellect would stop allowing me even this one indulgence. My embittered sense of the world would eventually refuse to allow me even the little comfort of believing in their incorporeal existence. *God is dead,* I told myself. *Athena is dead. They are all dead and gone and you, Jake, you are left to struggle.*

A long life ahead of me seemed a curse, an

inescapable sentence, and I saw myself as an old man, skin withered like the seed of a peach but with no power to bloom into fruit, into flesh. I was tired. Weary. Not even eighteen years old, I felt spent. No amount of coaxing could convince me that my best years were not behind me.

At one point in my freshman year, a college coed named Kelly was keeping vigil over me in my dormitory bed, holding me on my side with her own thin body. She aimed my face over my grey-chewing-gum-ed trash can each time I would puke rancid-tasting vomit; she had developed the singleness of mind one sometimes gets in drunkenness and made a semi-lucid decision: she would not let me drown tonight. She listened as I raved about pictures and cannons, boats and night stars, repeating the action of aiming my face over the can, wiping it with an old T-shirt, settling back again against my torso, her legs dangling over the bed. Then I said something about living *so long*. About how many more years it would be before I might heal. This girl Kelly, whom I barely knew, looked at me in dismay, her pretty features almost coming into focus before my bleary eyes.

"Jake, it's only been five months. It's still September," she had said to me, looking searchingly at my dimmed features.

I had paused then, considered this new information very seriously. It had not been half a year since they had died. What felt like an eternity had not yet filled the space of six months. If this was true, and I had no reason to disbelieve this sun-tanned girl sitting up on my bed, I might still have a chance. It was a slow and deliberate line of reasoning, protracted by the alcohol still hampering my senses, and it resulted in producing just enough hope to get me through that first quarter at Cal Poly. For the next two and a half months, I disappeared among thousands of students and spent almost every weekend obliterated. Self-medication nearly killed me, but it might have saved my life, too.

I wrote volumes about my distress, my disillusionment, the ways I had been disappointed by what Athena had called the *Divine*. I felt that she, too, had been let down by the *Divine*, that entity she had spoken of with such wistfulness. Indeed, in our limitations as beings who occupy physical bodies, we cannot begin to fathom an existence superior to the one we know; the one that connects us to this earth, to all the other corporeal beings who have loved us into our selves. What is human and physical limns our entire conception of self, bounds it with the flesh, whispers its perfection, denies the impermanence of such a shell. For a young person, death is an interruption. An unnatural twist of events. It is an end. A full stop. What else within such limitation?

I know and you know, I can see through the window... But could I? Perhaps I had simply been writing about Kenya's bedroom window, through which I had scrambled countless times, to crash-land on her plush carpet—that last time, into Athena's arms. Such memories carried physical pain. That burning sensation inside my ribcage. I let them smolder there.

I went this way, you said before...The punctuation was all. Had she *said* it before, or had she been *this way* before? The comma, or its absence, meant everything. And what *way*? The way of love? Of death? How? Questions like these haunted my waking hours, filled sleepless nights. I felt there was something to know.

"Oh," I would sometimes say. Nothing more. It was an expression of my despair. Of my longing. My mouth, in uttering it, made the shape of my unfaith. Dark cave of my undoing. *Oh.*

And then, in the spring of that next year, there was a little light. Just a little. I didn't even know where it came from. It corresponded to a few things. I had begun to surf a bit, for instance. And I wasn't losing myself in alcohol every chance I got. I wasn't kissing and ditching every girl I wandered into in a drunken oblivion, as if I was searching for someone and thought I might find her in their lips. I was running—a lot. I would sometimes run ten miles at a time, out Highway One toward Morro Bay in the heat and yellow stillness of the chaparral landscape. I would play recordings of Roethke, e.e. cummings, Bogan and Frost—reading their poetry aloud—on my yellow Discman. My running shoes pounded the asphalt in rhythm with their iambs, their heavy syllables, as I went.

A degree of light emerged, the dark undercurrent of my sadness not leaving, but slipping gently beneath this new sensation. There was some little disturbance on the surface of my mourning: a water bug. A dragonfly. I couldn't name it, but it was a quickening, a lightening, a new breath to take. I took it greedily, clenching my side-ache as I ran. Breathing the language of others, filling my lungs with something more universal than my own sadness, my own suffering. Such an act is a thing of beauty. Inhaling something greater than the self, becoming willing to open oneself to the sadness, the suffering, of others. And to their happiness, too...acknowledging that it might spill into your own experience of this unpredictable life. One day. One day.

I would see Angela occasionally...around campus or at a party. At the beach. I was increasingly aware of the change that was visibly occurring in her. She seemed to open like a lotus blossom, one petal at a time, so that finally, she was nearly unrecognizable from the tight little bud that had come into my teenage life so peripherally and had become inextricably entwined with my devastation. To separate Angela at all during those early years from my anguish, from the obliteration of my entire belief system, would have been superhuman. It would have been too much to ask.

But I would sometimes see her out in the water, taking off deeper, riding bigger, more threatening waves than I felt inspired to face. She would go on weekend surf trips with buddies to Santa Barbara, Point Loma, back up to Santa Cruz, and always return with the wide, salty smile I had come to know well. It carried in it something of the real. She was the only person at Cal Poly who had known Athena and the twins. I would sometimes seek them in her face, and what I found there, though nothing of the girls I sought, reassured me from afar. She was growing lovelier, Angela, and something in her gentle ease reminded me of home.

In my room in Hanover Hall, and in each of the subsequent domiciles of my undergraduate years, I had set Athena's photo on my desk; it was a black and white I had taken for photo class our senior year. By grad school I had acquired a frame that was black and adorned with a host of tiny white seashells, and now they framed Athena's complicated smile. Her smile daily suggested an alternate ending that could have been mine, had I (or someone else) just made the choice on the right page. By the time I was twenty-three and graduating with a master's degree in English literature from Cal Poly, San Luis Obispo, it was more a matter of habit to keep that photo visible. Still, I knew about the meaning we attach to things, especially things that represent what we have lost. In some shamefaced part of myself, I knew that I was still living like I was Athena's boyfriend.

On my last night in SLO, Angela invited me to a party at her house. She had worked her way through her undergraduate and master's degrees, switched her major to psychology somewhere along the way, and was heading off to U.C. Berkeley to earn her doctorate. Tonight she was celebrating with friends, her parents having checked themselves into some themed room at Madonna Inn for a celebration of their own. Their only daughter, through trial and triumph, had finished the first legs of her college journey. This called for a night in an all-rock grotto room, or maybe the Western or Merry-Go-Round suite. I laughed to think of them drinking champagne, dancing in the antiquated ballroom, dining on velvet cushions in a private celebration of parental success.

Tonight, Angela was adorned with that light that had begun to creep into my consciousness, and as I stood on the balcony of her condo, I allowed myself the small pleasure of watching her through golden-framed windows as she moved through the party. She wore a backless brown dress, the tiny freckles on her shoulder blades a sweet little temptation. Her glasses had long ago been replaced by contact lenses, and her smile was full of ease and yes, even a little grace. I laughed a little at the way she postured, adult-like, offering hors d'oeuvres to her guests, slipping locks of her light brown hair behind her ears to reveal little gold hoops that matched the hoops of her irises. She was changed, that was sure, and I watched, too, as a muscular young man, maybe two or three years her senior, slid his arm around her waist, kissed the side of her head and laughed at some joke that was beyond my hearing.

By the time Angela joined me outside on the balcony, having slipped soundlessly out the sliding glass door in her bare feet, I had turned my back on that congregation of vaguely familiar strangers. Angela and I had not really hung with the same crowd in college, and I had come to her party as a gesture that had in it a kind of finality. I didn't know what it was I meant to say, but there was something to be said; before we parted ways, I thought I might create a space in which it could be spoken.

I was leaning with my forearms on the railing, contemplating the shadows of maple trees in the distance, the movement of leaf against night sky. I was quietly drinking some sophisticated imported beer and dreaming this way, when her voice at my ear startled me.

"Hey there. You having any fun?" she said lightly, barely nudging me with her hip and settling in a similar position on the railing at my side.

"Oh yeah, it's good. Great condo, by the way." I knew I sounded lame, but I needed to warm up a bit.

"Thanks. Yeah, we really enjoyed living here." For a moment I wondered if 'we' meant her and the guy with the biceps, but I declined to ask. "Weird without the furniture," she added and by way of explanation: "Last night here. I'm sleeping at my folks' tonight."

I smiled at the image of the three Wilders tucked into the Austrian Suite or the Oriental Fantasy room. "Ah," I said, gesturing toward the empty interior, "it's good for a party. Plenty of space."

"Yeah…for the break dancing." Angela had always been good at introducing levity in tense moments, whether by design or not. I had forgotten that about her. We both laughed a little and fell silent. Our personal reveries were interrupted by a squeal from inside and subsequent peals of hearty laughter. When I looked at Angela again, she was scanning my face.

"When do you leave?" she asked.

"Monday," I answered. I was moving to Hawai'i. It was a decision I had reached in the space of about two weeks. It was simply the best solution for the aimlessness I was destined to feel upon exiting school with a graduate degree in English literature and no definitive plans for my future. I hadn't wanted to get a teaching credential, but I wasn't really ready for a doctoral program. I mostly wanted to surf, which was quickly becoming my favorite pastime (I guess you could say I was a late bloomer).

"Wow. That's soon," she said, turning back toward the maples. "I can't believe you're moving to Hawai'i. People really do that, huh?"

"Yeah, it's pretty crazy. I just met this guy who

teaches at a prep school on the Big Island. We got to talking and one thing led to another. I get housing and food. It seems easy…and fun. I figure I'll teach English Lit to overachievers for a while and see where it leads. It sort of feels like postponing my entrance into that ever-hovering 'real world' they always talk about, you know?"

"Yeah, I know all about that," she said.

"Right. PhD program. You've got your own version of escapism going on. We're not so different, you and I. Except while I'm surfing the Kona Coast, you'll be kicking ass on a bunch of hapless undergrads and researching your brains out. Berkeley's pretty nuts. You ready for that kind of pressure?"

"Yeah," she said thoughtfully, "I think I am."

"Yeah. You are." Angela was a go-getter. That I knew. She would be fine, and I probably would be, too. For a moment we both gazed out over the trees and the star-studded sky that draped itself over them. Without warning, she turned to me and spoke.

"You miss them still," she said. It wasn't exactly a question.

"I do," I admitted, and we were both quiet for a bit. I could hear her breathing, long and even, could see something moving behind her eyes.

"There are so many ways that night could have been different, you know? I go over it in my head, but—"

"Don't," I interrupted. "It only makes it harder. I've done it for six years now."

"You dated much?" she asked. I shook my head 'no.' It had not been for lack of opportunity, and there had been the occasional one-night-stand, but I had just not seen any reason to give myself to another person. Indeed I had done that long ago, as a boy, and never reclaimed myself. It was not so mysterious. I had no illusions, and I wasn't prone to drama. I had avoided having a girlfriend. That was all. And then, without planning to speak at all, I found myself explaining:

"I know she's gone. I should let go. There's an order to grieving. I've read all about it. I'm moving through it at a slower pace than some—but at least I can locate myself on the chart, you know?"

I paused for a moment. Someone was smoking cloves in the lot below us, and its sweet, pungent scent was rising through the still night air. I had more to say.

"We were just kids, but…I don't really feel any different. And my feelings for her haven't changed. And the guilt—of not giving her a love poem, of not suggesting that she and I stay back and make out in the hammock instead of taking a ride in the boat, of not being better for her. It intensifies the memory. It makes her so perfect. Crystalline. I know she had faults, but you know, I can't remember a single one. No one can compete with that. Perfection only happens in death. How can I attach myself to the living?"

"Yes, how can you?" My verbosity had surprised us both, I think, but I thought I heard a little bitterness in Angela's voice when she said this. It was an equivocal concession, at best. I looked at her then, saw her searching for something in that tree line, in the arch of sky above it.

"You know I don't blame you," I said magnanimously. "I never did."

"I know, Jake," was her simple response. "And it wasn't my fault." She said it gently, firmly. She straightened up then, smoothed the front of her silky dress, smiling a little sadly, I thought.

"I should get back in there. Check on the cheese log or something." The levity again. Bless her.

"God, you're so mature," I teased. She smiled and wrinkled her nose at the thought.

"It was good to see you, Jake," she said, precipitating a good bye I wasn't entirely sure I was ready for. There was no reason I could see to resist it, though, and the boyfriend had come to usher her inside, casting me what felt rather annoyingly like a glance of benign sympathy.

"You, too, Angela. Really." And there was a moment it would have been natural for us to hug or kiss or something, but instead I lifted my bottle to her idiotically and took a big gulp. She, with a puzzled little expression on her face, took the extended hand of her stalwart beau and was inside again before I knew what had happened.

I stood for a moment, feeling dejected and strange. It was a weird goodbye—an unnatural parting—but it was the one I had created. I had rather developed a habit of lying in the beds I made, so I took the last swig of my beer and chose to exit by the balcony steps. It was easier than making my way back through the party, which seemed to have tripled in size since I had first passed through it.

That was almost an end. There are so many of those in life…almost ends. And then there are breaks—from people. I would break from Angela for a long time…but not until after one more absurd phone call. Her party had left me a little uncertain. I had thought there was something to say; I had said something indeed. But was it the thing?

Nine

Jake

My first nights in my apartment in the Kamalani Dormitory on the Hawai'i Island Academy campus were pretty funny. I had arrived on Island without a car and had unwittingly incurred a fifty-dollar cab fee for a ride up the hill from Kona. I had not realized the distance between the airport and the town of Waimea, or that most of that distance was across a lava field spanning the entire coastline. I spent most of that ride feeling as if I had landed on the moon, rather than in a tropical island paradise.

I arrived in Waimea to howling trade winds and a fine, sideways rain typical of the upcountry summer weather; it was at least ten degrees cooler than it had been on the coast and the H.I.A. campus was tucked in to rolling hills veiled by a heavy, grey mist on all sides. The one redeeming aspect of my day was a vibrant vertical rainbow that came and went all afternoon and appeared, finally, to land on the playing fields just beyond the dormitory.

As I had arrived three days before the start of the summer session, the campus was deserted, the regular school year teachers already having cleared out for their summer travels and the summer school teachers not having yet arrived. It was decided by the Director of Development that I could temporarily "rent" what I later came to know as the "Green Machine," a 1979 Dodge station wagon with faux wood paneling. The car had been bequeathed to the school as a tax write-off by some alumnus or their parents. As the campus was a good mile and a half of windy, uphill highway from town, acquiring my own vehicle was going to be an early priority. Grateful for the five-dollar-a-day Green Machine, I did wish its windows could close and perhaps that I could come and go from campus a little less conspicuously. As I would eventually learn, no manner of inconspicuous vehicle would ever mitigate the fishbowl quality of living on a high school campus, and luckily, I would grow to love life at H.I.A. for all of its aspects, including this transparency.

The few boxes I had mailed to myself had preceded me and were on the floor and kitchen table of my apartment when I entered, led by a young girl who looked to be about eighteen and had met me in the parking lot. She was the Summer Programs office assistant named Liza, working until her departure to college in August. She had dangled my apartment key on the end of her finger as she slinked her way in rubber slippers over the stone walkway to my front door. Apparently I had not been expected for two more days, and there was no faculty member or administrator to greet me. Just Liza in her shorts and a pale tank top that rose just enough above the smooth mound of her belly to reveal a silver piercing. I thanked Liza and more or less kept her from entering the apartment with the strategic positioning of my own body, my giant backpack and my surfboard bag.

"Thank you, then, uh—Liza," I said, struggling slightly in the doorway. "I've got it from here."

She stood for a moment with her hands on her narrow hips, lips parted in a too familiar smile that made me avert my eyes. Her brown hair was streaked with sun, and I tried not to notice the exact place it hit the small of her back as she turned to go.

"Okay, Mr. Jameson," she had said with a shrug, and meandered away down the walkway toward the offices. They were obscured from view by a rock wall and a little line of cypress trees I later learned had been recently planted by the math teacher. He had also, in his early days at the school, planted the mile of pines that spanned the distance behind the dormitories and turned up the hill in a leaning procession. These green figures lining a near vertical path up the hill would become an integral part of the idyllic image of the campus that still lingers in my mind's eye.

"Jesus," I had said under my breath to no one in particular, as Liza made her exit. I stepped inside then and surveyed my new abode where, little did I know, I would live for the next twelve years. It was a rather crude apartment with the kind of carpet you see in airports; it smelled a bit like damp lumber, sunscreen and pine cleaning solution. Rough wooden cabinets housed the most basic of essentials: four plates, four cups, a few pots and pans, a colander, a cheese grater, and so on. The bathroom was cramped, and a stackable washer and dryer could be reached from the toilet. The bedding was a retro-style aloha print comforter over dorm-issue sheets, and there was rattan lounge furniture upholstered in Hawaiian print fabric before a stone fireplace. It was perfect, really, for the bachelor that I was. Nothing fancy.

It was the view that made me catch my breath. By now the mist had lifted to the west, and I could see all the way to the ocean. It was a view that was not to change for all my years at H.I.A. and one that would provide the backdrop for my life on the Big Island. I would spend those years comfortably ensconced by a little high school campus skirting the famous Parker Ranch.

By then it was sunset, and the sun and accompanying clouds were staining the sky the of a blood-orange. The sun was just touching down on the watery horizon. The ocean was a deep blue line and comprised one of the layers of striated landscape visible from the balcony I would eventually learn to call a lanai. Between the sea and me: a porous black layer of hardened lava, the yellow grasses of the lowlands, the pale green of Waimea's pastureland—the Kohala Mountains rising to the North and appearing to tumble headlong toward all of this. I stood surveying the scene, increasingly aware of the silence surrounding me, when there came a small knock at the door leading into the dormitory.

It was Liza again, this time with a cube-shaped box resting on her hip, her brown arm draped over it casually. "Hi," she said, smiling widely.

"Uh—hi."

Stretching out behind her I could see a long hall of dormitory rooms that would soon enough be filled with smelly, loud, irreverently endearing boys; for now, the place was haunted by a certain nothing that sent a little shiver up my spine. Outside, it had begun to sprinkle again, but I would learn soon enough that the rain in Waimea isn't the kind that gets things wet. Just then it was making Liza rather glisten in a way that made *me* feel very uncomfortable. I cleared my throat uneasily as she walked past me with her offering and set it on my kitchen counter.

"You're going to need this, Mr. Jameson," she said easily, taking her time and looking around the room at my boxes and things. Perhaps in response to my quizzical expression, she explained: "Rice cooker. Dining hall's closed until Sunday. That's when the kids arrive."

"Oh, right," I said, though I had never used a rice cooker in my life.

"Rice is inside," she added. "Hawaiian staple."

"Thanks," I said dumbly.

Still making her way around the room, meandering among the boxes, she asked, "Is there a Mrs. Jameson?" Still, that smirk on her face. Still that slight sense of panic in my stomach.

"No, uh, not yet!" I said. "Close, though," I added emphatically, putting my thumb and forefinger together to indicate just how close. Liza had already lost interest, though, and was making her way back toward the door as I considered my reckless little lie and its ridiculous accompanying gesture. She slid a finger beneath her tank top strap absently, pulling it back onto her shoulder. She glanced over it again as she exited.

"Alright, Mr. Jameson. I'm in Mr. Richards' office if you need me for anything. Classes on Monday."

"Right," I said awkwardly. "Got it," I added for no reason at all, tripping on a box on my way to close the door behind her. I'm sure I heard her giggle as she sauntered down the darkening hall.

From my doorway there was a straight shot into the common room at the far end of the hall. You could just see the corner of the ping-pong table that would be the center of post-study hall dormitory activity on the weeknights to come. During holidays, when the dorm was as freakishly quiet as it was now, empty of our pubescent charges, it would become the venue for some wicked matches of beer pong among the younger faculty. I quickly learned that a boarding school teaching gig was, to a twenty-something male fresh out of school, a perfect excuse to extend his college years indefinitely. Just when he decided to give it up for a more 'normal' existence, a handful of vacancies for the upcoming school year would open up the promise of an incoming coed from Mount Holyoke or Barnard, and he would stick around to see how the staffing panned out. Of course, there was a pecking order, too; newbies were not just free game to all, but on the off chance that their number might be up and that the new twenty-four year old Spanish teacher might turn out to be fabulously Shakira-esque, young men found themselves sticking around for more years than they ever intended to.

It was so important to me to assert myself as an 'adult' in those first years at H.I.A.; I made a note to myself to always wear a tie to classes. I even considered growing some variety of facial hair. For me, and more so because of what I had experienced my senior year in high school, the six years that separated me in age from these seniors was an eternity. For them—and they were very astute—I was a mere boy.

After Liza had gone for the second time, I took a seat on my little couch and put my feet up on a glass-topped rattan coffee table. I pulled my sweatshirt hood onto my head and rested with arms folded, quietly contemplating my move. If I hated it I could always bail after summer school. Breaking my contract for the school year was not going to ruin me; not like I really wanted to be a teacher. I wondered how long it had been since anyone had lit a fire in the fireplace and listened for some time to the sound the wind made in its hollows.

After a while, I considered my departure from California, how it turned out my mother and I were both leaving it. Her rocker boyfriend had finally chosen a port in which to settle and marry; Santa Cruz was not it, my mother not the bride. She hadn't acted surprised, only tired, her cosmetically improved eyes refusing to let her disappointment show in her expression.

I said goodbye to her out in front of the familiar yacht harbor house, her moving van idling in the driveway. As she began to drive away, she had stopped abruptly, said, "Oh!" and held up a finger for me to wait just a minute. After some time digging in her handbag, she had produced a yellowed envelope with my name written across it in Angela's neat hand.

"It was in the glove box of Phonso's car," she said. "I found it when I was cleaning out my things." The Jaguar. Graduation day. I took the envelope from my mother, who was now leaning into my pickup at the window, and put the envelope on the passenger's seat. She kissed me on the cheek, her musky perfume swirling into the cab.

"Bye, Mom," I said simply.

"Goodbye, Jake."

Now on the couch in my new apartment, I took the envelope from my bag, held it in my hands, remembering the moment it had been given to me on our high school graduation day. Angela. Such earnestness in her manner, in her gift. I still had the Tara figurine and had even brought it to Hawai'i with me. It was one of the few items that graced my dresser wherever I went: an alarm clock, Athena's photo, my mother's rosary, generally hung from a mirror or a thumbtack, and Tara.

The idea of Tara, goddess of feminine compassion, sharing a space in the world with a symbol of my mother, was all the irony I needed in life. It made me smile sometimes. But the card.

I had forgotten putting the card into the glove box of the Jaguar, and it had sat there under registration papers, sunglasses, extra sunscreen...for six years now. What might she have written then? What words did Angela have for me? Had they required a response that I had unwittingly neglected to provide? I knew my hesitation to open it now was silly, but there was some little fear there. As if it held a portal back to that moment, so achingly real, now gently obscured by time and the clemency of fading memory.

When I finally opened it, I saw that it was adorned on the front with a Chagall painting. This card, real, in my hand, from Angela. And inside, her handwriting again:

I am the man in the suit (see my sad little smile) and you are the woman in pink. Floating. Perhaps they are there, Jake. I hope you find them. Love to you, Jake Jameson. On this important day. I miss them, too.

Ever, Angela

She was referencing the painting, of course, but she had touched a nerve.

"Hmmmmm," I had said, sitting back on the uncomfortable cushion of my rattan couch. Here was Angela's recognition of the wild hope that had filled my heart in those days. The question that burned inside my ribcage still. I wanted to believe the girls were there, somewhere beyond this plane, hovering and alive in a way that transcended the body. Perhaps. Perhaps. I looked for them in various landscapes, sought Athena's voice in certain songs; there were moments I was sure I sensed them, especially in the beginning.

Once I had thought I felt Athena looking over my shoulder as I scanned the sea near her parents' house. I had closed my eyes and held very still, so as not to disturb her, as if she were a dragonfly and might dart away at any sudden move. I collected her with my breath, held her with my desperate intention, for a single protracted minute. Then she was gone, and I could not be sure I had not conjured that feeling myself, manufactured the dream of her presence with my wayward desire. There was always reason that told me my imagination had a life of its own and warned me not to trust it. But then, those were the days when imagination and actual creation occupied separate spheres in my consciousness. Before I allowed the two to merge in the web of my belief and teach me about the fluidity of the *real.*

As to my friends who had died, I could never confirm that in fact, something of their essences continued without the bodies that had held them for eighteen years on this earth and had anchored them to the visible, tangible world of concrete experience.

So often we miss opportunities to connect. We resist and resist what is most healing in the world, and in our desperate search for the dead, we deny the living. I didn't know why I resisted Angela's compassion. Why I continued on some level to resist it. It was as if I knew that every pixel of a whole picture of life might be found in her face, if I just looked long enough, let my eyes blur, come into focus again without their inculpating lens. But I could not sustain that gaze. As a boy, seventeen years old and broken, I looked away. I had looked away again on her balcony that night of her party. Even before I finished reading the card, I knew that I would ultimately do the same again.

I am the man in the suit (see my sad little smile) and you are the woman in pink. Floating.

I closed the card again to have a better look at the painting. It was from a series of self-portraits Chagall had done, the back of the card said. In this one, also his wife. The man stands in a black suit, floppy white collar protruding; he is on a grassy hill, the accoutrements for a ful picnic in the foreground at his feet. His wife is floating above him, like a kite. He holds her right hand, as if it were a kite string; she drifts in a pale sky above green hills that roll into green houses. There is an ethereal-looking pink house, or perhaps a church, framed nearly in the center of the painting but far in the background. The man is smiling an indolent, fearless smile suggestive of patience. Contentment, even. *Her* mouth is pursed with her waiting, but there is a small smile there, as well. Neither is distressed by her apparent inclination toward flight, and the lone blossoming bough of a tree leans into the picture at the left…the suggestion of something rooted, just outside the frame.

I sat poring over that painting and those words for some time. Well into the hours of darkness. There were things suggested there that I would not fully grasp for years to come, but I had enough sense at that young age to grapple fiercely with them that night and to later purchase the print of "The Walk" and hang it prominently in that very living room. For the moment, I picked up the rotary phone that was plugged into the wall next to me. I had to dig in my wallet for the little folded paper containing Angela's number.

I waited impatiently as the phone rang six, seven times and thought for sure I would get an answering machine. I quickly tried to devise a not-so-lame message. And then suddenly, her voice on the other end of the line.

"Hello?" she said, a little breathless.

"Angela?"

"Yeah…Jake?

"Yeah, it's Jake…"

"Oh my god, you just interrupted the biggest air microphone session. I almost didn't hear the phone over the music—and then I couldn't find the phone under all the packing material! What are you doing? Are you in Hawai'i?"

"Uh—yeah. I'm here. I mean, in Hawai'i. I arrived today."

"Everything okay?" she asked, her voice slightly tinged with concern.

"Yeah, everything's great. So…what are you up to?"

"I told you. I was in concert when you called. Violet, my tabby cat, was seriously enjoying my Journey lip sync into my hairbrush. I'm setting up my new place in Berkeley. It's late at night, you know. What time is it there?" She sounded happy. Excited.

"I don't know, maybe ten."

"Yeah, I'm three hours ahead of you," she said.

"Oh, sorry. I wasn't even thinking—"

"No worries," she said lightly, "you happened to call on the first night of the tour. The roadies are all crashed out, but Violet is still watching. Buster, too. Remember Buster?"

"The stuffed dog?"

"Yeah, you remember!" It took me a moment to follow her playful line of conversation. I pictured her standing on her bed in pink fuzzy slippers and pajamas, singing into her hairbrush the lyrics of "Don't Stop Believing." We were not so grown up, I thought, and it was a bit of a comfort.

"This is the first time I've not had a housemate," Angela chattered. "It's great! I feel like I can just spill into any room I want. All this space is mine, you know?"

"Yeah," I said rather unconvincingly, "it's great." I looked around my own dismal apartment and thought I should probably be doing what Angela was doing. There were posters here somewhere. Some knick-knacks from travels I'd taken. A blanket I could toss over the hideous overstuffed chair in the corner.

"You sure everything is okay?" she asked again. Was I so transparent? Thoughts darted around in my head, flirting with the prospect of vocalization: the card, Angela's words, the rice cooker girl in hot shorts, the long, echo chamber of a hall outside my door.

"Yeah. God. Sorry! I don't know what's up with me. Uh, I should let you go," I said.

"It's okay, I mean—"

"Maybe you'll have to take a Hawaiian vacation sometime," I blurted absurdly. Talk about left field. I took the receiver and pretended to stab myself with it. I rushed it back to my ear when I heard her voice respond.

"Yeah, maybe I will," she said simply, as if there was nothing out of the ordinary in me inviting her to my house after virtually six years of more or less avoiding contact—oh yeah, and one bizarrely strained party conversation. It had been exactly four days since I had stood on her balcony and given no indication that I was interested in ever speaking to her again.

"Yeah, I mean, I think it'll be better when the kids get here. The boarding students arrive on Sunday," I said, still skirting my own invitation.

There was a slight pause."Is it like you thought it would be, Jake?" she asked rather timidly.

"I guess I don't know what I thought," I answered, honest for perhaps the first time that night and not unaware of the implications of her question. "I—I think it's easiest not to have expectations, you know?"

"Yeah, I guess. Can you see the ocean?" she asked then, expectantly. I made my way over to the lanai where I had flung the doors open wide and left them that way in spite of the chill they admitted. I struggled a bit with the long cord of the phone as I squinted into the darkness.

"I can see this fine line between the black lava and the dark blue sky. I'm pretty sure that's the sea." I had succeeded in getting enough slack in the cord to stand upright. Now I stood there, wordlessly watching that line.

"Sounds nice," she said rather wistfully. "It's good to hear your voice, Jake."

"You, too, Angela. I guess I'll let you go."

"Yeah, I—take care, okay?"

"Yeah, okay. Bye," I said back.

In almost a whisper, she said it too: "Bye."

It is sometimes like that when an end occurs—or a long hiatus begins. Without anyone even realizing it's happening. I suppose Angela got really wound up in her doctoral work, teaching university classes; and there was still the business of the boyfriend, whose name I had finally learned was Brock. Figured he would have a soap opera name. He adored her, I knew, and he was setting up his law practice in the Bay Area to be near her. Angela was grounded, rooted like a tree. She was physical, *real* in a way I could not have even hoped to be in those days. And truly beautiful. She deserved to be happy. I convinced myself of all this and more when I hung up the phone that first night in Hawai'i, and it was these dialogues I set up in my head that prevented me from calling her again. Nearly twelve years would pass before we spoke again. Twelve years that were the difference between a grieving boy and a man who would deny his boyhood grief.

My second morning at H.I.A. I drove the Green Machine into town under a blue sky shifting with rain-laden clouds. I managed to compose myself after having nearly lost my life (and decimated the Green Machine) crossing a tiny curved bridge at the same time as a bread truck. I made another note to self, regarding the Waiaka Bridge. Though no sign indicated it was a one lane crossing, most local drivers treated it as such, and traversing it simultaneously from the opposite direction was more or less taking one's life into one's own hands. Or worse, placing it in those of other drivers.

The little stream that was on one day dry and on another day raging with water from rainforest precipitation, wound gently through the town. Twice the highway that doglegged its way through Waimea crossed it: once at that crazy turn near campus, and once at the main stoplight, for there were only two. I was surprised to see just how much of a ranching community this was, and I noticed a small rodeo arena on my way. Horses grazed in verdant pastures on either side of me; these were now and again graced with rainbows, and it occurred to me after a few weeks of living there that I could see rainbows every day of my life if I chose to stay in Waimea. It was something to consider. The roadside was dotted with little plantation style homes and larger ranch houses leaning under that shifting light, their yards manicured by the odd goat or donkey. I passed a small gas station, a couple of island style "plate lunch" joints, a roadside stand offering fresh Waimea strawberries and "huli huli chicken."

On my right as I drove into town, I saw a shopping center painted much like a red barn, its u-shaped structure protecting a grassy courtyard flanked by hibiscus flowers and birds of paradise. I was attracted by a sign that said, "Waimea Java," and bore the simple outline of a coffee cup with steam rising from it. I made a hard right. As I walked toward the screen door of the coffee shop, I noticed an upstairs apartment with a hand-painted sign in the window. It appeared to be both a residence and a business, and the sign said, "Clairvoyant Healings and Readings." It was adorned with a sun and a moon, and the curvy lettering was in purple.

Inside, I nearly collided with a woman who was stirring cream into her tea at the tiny station near the door. Everything was near the door inside this cramped little coffee shop, but I liked it instantly. The woman smiled at me from beneath a mop of salt and pepper curls and shifted to let me by. There were three little round tables, two of which were occupied by the two men I would see there for years to come. One sipped his coffee and held a newspaper away from his face in order to read it without glasses, and the other, whose fifty-something head was covered with uncannily thick white hair, held a small white dog on his lap, as he sipped his coffee.

"What can I do for you?" asked a young girl from behind the counter, beaming. At about five feet tall, her ample figure resembled the Venus of Willendorf, and her smile was broad and comfortable. She leaned casually on the counter and waited for me to speak. The other three people had more or less stopped what they were doing and appeared to be awaiting my order, too.

"I'll have a latté. Large, please," I said, squirming a bit under their mild scrutiny. Behind me, the woman was preparing to go, her long flowery garment appearing to follow her at some distance.

"Bye Phyllis. Have a good day," said the girl behind the counter. The words "Waimea Java" rippled acrossthe front of her apron as she waved.

"See you tomorrow, Daphne. Bye, Billy. Howard." The man with the dog nodded his acknowledgement and rather grunted, his mouth full of scone, but the other man waved gaily and called to her.

"Have a nice day, Phyllis!"

"You too, Howard," she said, smiling back at him. Her eyes passed over me again, too, and for a moment I felt naked. It was a momentary feeling of vulnerability and it passed as quickly as it had come. She seemed to wink at me as she went out, but I couldn't be sure. I watched her pass in front of the shop and ascend the staircase leading up to the mysterious little compartment above.

"That'll be three-fifty," said the little Venus.

"Sorry!" I said, finally handing my money to her, though there was no need to apologize for anything. I shook my head at myself and tried to shake off the slight disorientation I was feeling.

"No problem. You Mr. Jameson?" she asked, which was disconcerting enough without the renewed interest of Howard and Billy behind me.

"Yes, I..."

"You're the new English teacher. I'll be in your Senior Seminar class in the fall." Extending her hand cordially, she introduced herself: "I'm Daphne Roberts."

I took her hand and relaxed a little. "Nice to meet you, Daphne."

"Small Big Island," she said, intuiting my thoughts.

"Yeah, I guess so," I said, smiling sheepishly. Her continued smile and the gazes of the two men and "Bobo" the dog made me uncomfortable again.

"Well, gotta' go!" I said, gesturing to the pile of books I had brought in with me. I nearly dropped them as I tried to transfer them from the counter to the one free table and scoffed at the illusion under which I was clearly functioning: that once I was seated at my table, not four feet from any of the three people in the room, I would have some level of privacy.

Just then Phyllis breezed back into the shop and

began opening another packet of sugar to add to her tea.

"Incorrigible sweet tooth," she explained to me, winking for real this time. I held up the handful of sugar packets I'd grabbed on my way in and smiled sympathetically. As if something had just occurred to her, she turned to me at my table and extended her hand.

"Phyllis Appleton," she announced.

"Jake Jameson," I returned. "New in town."

"No!" she said, feigning surprise.

"That obvious, huh?" I said, laughing with her. "I'm a first year teacher at Hawai'i Island Prep."

"Well, welcome, Jake Jameson. I'm sure we'll see you around." Then she pulled a business card out of her pocket and set it down on my table. "In case you need me!" she said rather mysteriously and fairly glided out the door.

The card itself gave no indication of her line of work, no title or business name. Just her own name, Phyllis Appleton, in calligraphic script, and a phone number. I tucked it into my wallet and took my first sip of the best coffee in the world. It may have had to do with the fact that it came from my new favorite coffee shop, which also happened to be the only coffee shop in Waimea. Perhaps it was because I was drinking it later than usual and was beginning to feel my tardiness in the tightening of my skull. Whatever it was, it was heavenly.

It's hard to describe how incongruous these first impressions were with my imagined Hawai'i, and even more difficult to describe the way they enchanted me that first day and indeed, those first years, at H.I.A. It had something to do with the scent of Waimea rain on the grass and asphalt. The way the vibrant green hills rise and form a crescent around the town, how it spills open toward Mauna Kea, Hualalai and Mauna Loa, the three volcanoes rising in the distance. It was something about the little circuit that becomes one's daily movement through such a place, which would ever include Waimea Java, Howard and Billy, thereafter. Something about custom and habit and the comfort they provide.

I loved it all and had no need of more, though there

were nights we younger faculty would take the ride down the hill to the only nightclub for miles in those days. The place served also as a steak house, so we would go around sunset to sate our hunger for Parker Ranch beef and organic greens. Then we would dance and drink late into the night, burning off the steam of mountains of essays to grade and long evenings of dorm duty ahead of us and behind.

Eventually someone would drive home who was feeling a little less tipsy, perhaps a little more intrepid, than the others. I would hold my hand out the car window as we ascended toward Waimea, train my attention on the changing temperature as we moved away from the coast and toward our "mauka," or upcountry, home. The cool air was a gift after the heat of the coastal biome, and once home we would relish in a game of poker or gin rummy, the sliding doors open to the mist, until we dropped off to sleep in the wee hours of the morning.

Ten

Jake

I grew up there: a young teacher at H.I.A., teaching Camus and Dostoevsky to overachieving kids who lived a life many only dreamed of and which would channel them, at its close, into the universities of their choice. Most of them still experienced the strain of the teenage years; what is youth, after all, without a little angst? Still, they were hard pressed to find justification for their complaints in their surroundings, and those so inclined would settle moodily into artistic pursuits that represented their discomfort beautifully at least.

My classroom was a haven for these types, as I taught the creative writing classes and eventually revived the old literary magazine that had fallen off when some other young, energetic teacher had abandoned it, and H.I.A., years ago. It happened often that the school would burn through the "triple threat" energies of young teachers, keep them coaching and supervising and instructing every minute of every day until they had to make their escape. To a city on the "mainland" or back to their hometowns. Such was the nature of a boarding school.

I was the ideal candidate for longevity, and my administrators knew it. I was not susceptible to the common malaise of the other "newbies," who after a year or two would begin to wonder about the likelihood of finding a mate on this "godforsaken rock," this school "at the end of the earth." I loved the isolation of the island and sought for nothing beyond my experience there. I loved the island life, and I grew to love teaching. Guiding young souls to their own discoveries. Putting in the hands of a young person the poem or the story that might change their life, set them on some new course, if only for a time. I loved talking about books and about language, reminding my students that Kafka once asserted, "Writing is a form of prayer."

"Indeed it is the deepest expression of our hope in the Divine, even if it is only the divinity of the Self that our belief system embraces," I would say with great zeal. I knew that while there were a few who believed as I did and would jump aboard the "Jameson train" of poetry and lyricism for their time at H.I.A., most of them would be simply entertained by my passion, my zest, and find some kernel of truth in what I offered them. It was enough. Enough that someone might hear the whisper of Kate Chopin in her ear, or that the irreverence of Voltaire might inspire the latent satirist in an otherwise reticent boy.

The first several years, I filled my days with these satisfactions, surfed away weekend hours, gave myself to my students on the page, commenting ever in earnest on their creative and expository endeavors. I was the four-time winner of the Locatelli Meritorious Teaching Award, voted on by the students. Experience tells me now that one earns that award by being unequivocally theirs—belonging utterly to the students. Had I been in the throes of childrearing during those years, or even, like many of my colleagues, in love with a living being, I would have been theirs only to a certain degree, or only at certain intervals. But I belonged to the school I loved, to those kids, to the island.

Eventually, my private longings would sneak back into my life, but I managed to keep them at bay, for they had no place in this perfect world, where I felt in many ways invulnerable to fresh pain. I was content to live with the old pain in private, deal with it as it re-emerged and subsided again of its own accord. It seemed to have a life of its own, that ancient longing for what was no more. Never truly accepted by me, never integrated into my actual life, it could not be sustained. Had it been sustained, perhaps it could have been healed or transformed. As it was, it snuck up on me most unexpectedly, left me reeling, and receded again into shadowy memory, whispering its accusation to me as it went: *Coward*.

These bouts of remembered grief and solitary wandering would later result in writing sessions yielding four, five, six poems at a time. By now, however, my grief was organized, had cooled into a sort of gel, so that I could pour it slowly into the mold of formal verse: sonnet, villanelle, sestina. They weren't bad, those poems, contained as they were by structure and distanced as I was from the actual events that spawned them. They were often picked up by various literary magazines, and I began to amass a rather lengthy list of publications.

In public, in my community, I revealed only that part of me which celebrated life. It was easy enough. There were so many things I loved about this life: my students, the warm salt water populated by every manner of ful sea life, the view from my balcony. Surf and words. Kona coffee and a good metaphysical discussion. I was an island myself, or so I believed during the best times.

During the worst, I sequestered myself in my dormitory apartment, didn't answer the door or the phone, and became language. Nothing more. I literally lived in my journals at those times, let my beard cast its fine shadow on my jaw, lived on water and Longboard Lager. I would write poem after poem of often incomprehensible verse. I hid out in those poems. Flirted with the idea of revealing myself there, and then balked, gave myself over to mystery and often obscurity. *More garbage*, I thought.

Come Monday I would emerge a little bleary-eyed, a little sluggish, a distant light in my eyes. It would take me several hours to become re-accustomed to being in the land of the living. To moving amidst the real. After a day or so I would be back to myself, joking and laughing with my students and to colleagues. The ocean would rejuvenate me, and I would be vaguely relieved to know that another episode of my light madness was behind me.

It is the disparity between one's private self and one's public self that is so devastating, I think. One can be surrounded by so many loving and generous people, and if he has not truly shared with them, has carefully guarded what is lurking in the privacy of his soul, he will still know himself as completely alone. That kind of loneliness, the kind born of personally imposed distances in a sea of friends…this is the kind of loneliness that destroys.

In my dreams Pele laughed at me. We were one, she and I: we destroyed in order to create. But Pele, goddess of the volcano, never turned her destruction on herself. I seemed destined to, like the serpent that consumes its own tail, continue in the cycle of self-destruction, my creations never justifying the cost. How could a little poem ever compensate for the madness that swallowed me in those bouts of melancholy? Pele laughed, throwing back her fiery head, her enchanting eyes mocking me lovingly; then I would wake suddenly, sweat saturating my hair, my breath quick and shallow like a rabbit's.

My classroom was filled with surfing images, gaudy lamps I had gathered from garage sales in my resistance to fluorescent lighting, rugs and tapestries from around the world. I had gathered quite a collection in my summer travels over the years. On the largest wall hung a giant reproduction of a drawing of the young Samuel Taylor Coleridge. I always loved the way his center-parted hair lifted away from his fresh, young face in that image. Above his head floated apparently arbitrary language about limes and aphids, the absurdity of which only increased the appeal of the image for me.

The image floated above a large, laminated poster bearing a passage from Coleridge's own *Rime of the Ancient Mariner*:

> "Alone, alone, all, all alone,
> Alone on the wide wide sea!
> And never a saint took pity on
> My soul in agony.
>
> The many men, so beautiful!
> And they all dead did lie:
> And a thousand slimy things
> Liv'd on; and so did I."

My students never did guess at the proximity of these words to my own sentiments; it took even me years to identify the parallels. It seems incongruous, after all, for one surrounded by people as I was, to believe himself alone. And self-loathing is a thing one buries deeply. Also, regret. My students never saw it. Perhaps this is good teaching.

I had enough appreciation for life itself, for learning, and even love; these aspects of my consciousness worn on my sleeve, I was safe from the cognizance of darker ones housed within. Such a dramatic and "emo" expression of loneliness as found in these words from *Rime of the Ancient Mariner* was hard for my students to equate with any real life experience, though through our discussions and written explorations, I tried to help them do so.

While I ranked myself among the "thousand slimy things" that "liv'd on," I yet held out hope for a universal entity that, like the sea, might contain every grief, every joy at once, and must connect every living thing—even the one who has cast himself on the shore, alienated himself in earnest, though he is within earshot of the sighs of many others. It was the kind of hope that grows out of the habit of trying not to be swallowed by the more sinister human sentiments, and it was tenuous, at best, though I clung to it.

I knew, of course, that this unsteady hope could not sustain me, that keeping sixty or seventy students and a handful of colleagues a year at arm's length could not fulfill me in the end. I shared a lot with them, especially my students. But I never revealed my sense of being alone or the loss that still haunted me. I shared everything but that which made me human, for after all, I was no more than a teacher. No less. *That is all*. How does one bare a soul that atrophies in its isolation—out of habit one retreats from such an act. It is a cyclical habit. The illusion of intimacy is gained, the actual loneliness intensified.

And then came Lydia.

Eleven

Jake

"So your assignment, with these poems as models, is to write an unconventional love poem. Unconventional in that you are sure that nothing you include in it would ever appear in a greeting card. Unconventional in that it doesn't have to be romantic love. How about a love poem to your cat?" At this my students chuckled a bit. They were used to my frequent silliness as a means to very serious ends.

"Or to your grandmother? What about a love poem to the night sky? And if it is for a romantic love…how can you get at it, how can you approach it in a way that is new, wholly your own? Is it the way he falters before he takes your hand? The way she laughs as a stress response, even in situations where laughing is completely inappropriate? Maybe it's the way that mustard makes him sneeze. What? Make it fresh." I finished with a flourish of the paper I was holding and turned toward the whiteboard to post the assignment.

By now it was the fall of 2006. I was thirty-five and an old hand at drawing the creative matter from the young minds who flocked to my courses their senior year. The course itself had become rather a rite of passage at H.I.A. and was both dreaded and eagerly anticipated by the students in their final year of high school.

I referred often to the idea of the *Dreaming Place,* which exists in every mind, where our thoughts gallop unfettered by fear of judgment even from our selves. Some of those wild thoughts are clothed, some of them not, some of them four-footed, some of them two—all of them doing whatever they please. Perfect freedom exists in the *Dreaming Place,* I would tell my students, and with practice we can learn to fish our creative matter out of that place, set it on the page to reveal ourselves in new ways, express ourselves in fresh language that is wholly our own.

I saw myself as a kind of midwife of this language, of the poetry and stories that emerged from the pens of my students and which they later crafted in draft after draft of prose or verse. My job was to prepare the giver of this light, to use the Spanish metaphor, and coax the 'baby' down, usher it into the world and hold space for the 'mother,' be they male or female. To nurture it into the perfect thing it might become. Love had no small part in this process. My love of language and the creative process; their love of the newly born thing; a shared love of humanity and our arduous and timeless endeavor to express the self on a page.

It was Grace who caught me off guard with her question. She was definitely one of my favorites. Teachers say they don't have favorites, or they declare that *good* teachers don't, but they are lying. How could they not? We are human, after all. Like preferences for anything, a particular flavor of ice cream or roast of coffee, we develop little preferences for those students who make us smile or who demonstrate some little quality we admire. Sometimes they just remind us of some past version of ourselves or of people we love. Grace held up a mirror for me, showing me an image of my carefree, surfer self.

She was a tomboy of sorts, with long unruly hair that she usually kept in a bun at the back of her head. She was what locals call "hapa haole," which meant that she was half Hawaiian and half 'something European.' Grace hailed from the Kama'ole family, who had ranched on the Hawai'i Island for many generations now, and was the product of the union between a hotheaded Hawaiian cowboy and the blond-haired surfer girl he fell in love with. Since her parents had taken over the family ranch, Grace had become a boarder at H.I.A. In part, the decision was made to separate her from the grueling work of the ranch, which seemed not to be calling her, and to give her a decided focus on her education and related endeavors.

Grace wore board shorts pretty much every day and would sometimes lose a fair amount of salt water from her nose when she bent her head over her desk. At such times she would smile sheepishly and wipe it with the sleeve of her hoodie. It was all in the name of a good dawn patrol at "Beach Sixty-nines" or Paniau, for which one surfer day student or other would pick her up from the dorm around five in the morning and deliver her back to school with the salty residue of seawater dusting her temples, tangling her hair.

Grace always arrived to school within minutes of the bell, a surfboard still strapped to the top of the car. The shape of the board would always communicate, to those paying attention, the condition of the waves on that day. Long and wide with a single scag rising into the air like a shark fin meant long, slow, easy waves; a short, three-fin board with a deep curve meant fast, steep waves that took one's breath. Grace never wore a stitch of makeup and the knot of some swimsuit or other was always visible at the nape of her neck. She had a broad, happy smile, and a boyish little gait. Her poetry was a bit restrained, but she was a master at computer layout and had taken the helm of our literary magazine her junior year.

Now, she sat with bare feet in my Creative Writing Senior Seminar and waited patiently for me to call on her, her hand raised in the air.

"Yes, Grace?" I said.

"Mr. Jameson, do you have one? A love poem? You're published, right?" she ventured. She knew very well that I was published and was offering this information up for the benefit of the class, most of them new to me in these first few months of school. She had rather taken the self-appointed role of my secretary on the lit mag staff and was always reminding me of things, keeping me accountable. It landed somewhere between annoying and endearing. I hesitated to respond to her question, aware of various small affirmative noises from the rest of the class and a measurable increase in their attention on me.

"I've never published a love poem," I said. It was true—I hadn't. And then, something caused me to add, even after I had safely escaped the prompting, "But I *do* have one. *Only* one. And it *is* unconventional."

My heart began to accelerate its leisurely pace, and I found myself digging in my messenger's bag for my journal. In it I always carried the original copy of the poem I had written for Athena when I was a boy. The paper was worn along the lines it had first been folded, over seventeen years ago now. It had passed from journal to journal whenever I would reach the last page of a composition book, date it, and put it away, only to embark on a fresh one. I opened the paper now, careful not to tear it. I had not looked at it for many years. There was my handwriting, and below it the few doodles I had drawn while waiting for Athena to finish her art class that day. I had finally lost patience and summoned her to escape for a moment. She had slipped out of her painting smock and joined me in the spring sunlight outside Mrs. Girard's classroom. She had been so eager to see it, so happy. The memory was vivid, as were most of my memories of those last days with Athena, heightened now by my attention to this poem.

It is impossible to tell what will move us in any given moment to take a risk. Sometimes it is a risk we have avoided for long periods of time; sometimes it is one we have never contemplated before. On that day, my entire senior seminar raptly attentive to my every word, I chose to share something real. Prompted by a child, I took a risk I had never considered taking.

"Alright. Here's something I wrote when I was your age," I said. Several students sat up straighter in their chairs and stopped sketching in the margins of their notebooks, to gaze at me. I stood there with the paper in my hand, knowing well that I didn't need to read the words I had carried with me all this time. They had been sleeping there, just beneath the veil of consciousness. I felt the super-real begin to sift itself down into the real, the two realms of my life colliding softly as I prepared to read.

There was one student, named Lydia, whose gaze made me falter ever so slightly for just a moment. She was my best poet so far, a fairly quiet girl whose black hair shone like crow feathers, her dramatic bangs cut in a straight line across her forehead. While many mistook her for a local girl, her last name gave her away as a Greek beauty; not too many Papadakises on the island. She looked at me now with glossy black eyes like bottomless pools—blank, open. *Full of innocence,* I remember thinking.

I began by pretending to read, finding it easier to avert my eyes from the faces of my listeners:

"I know and you know..." By the third line I was looking up, no longer reading but looking each student in the eyes, offering something to them that I had never offered my past students.

"I went this way, you said before..." They listened with rapt attention, though with little understanding of the magnitude of this moment for me. I had given a million readings of my poetry, even read in London's Troubadour when I'd had work published in a little English journal called *Magma.* This was old hat, I told myself, but of course it was not.

As I delivered the last line, I could see Lydia, motionless, her eyes closed. She appeared to mouth the words with me as I spoke: "Jump the magic, it's up to you. Hurry up, the sky is blue," I concluded. I watched her then, trying to make sense of what I had perceived if only for a moment. But perceptions are tricky, so often pervaded by our desire, as it were, to connect with other human beings. To share what is in our hearts. Of course she had not mouthed the lines to my teenage poem. It was inadmissible. Easily dismissed.

There was silence in the room, but not because I had moved my students so very much with words that seemed, even to me, fairly superficial now. The poem itself lacked concrete language to anchor its abstraction. It was so light, I thought. It might lift off, take flight like an unmoored tent, so insubstantial was it compared with the weight of the real: these young bodies, these desks arranged in a circle, this rustic classroom with four walls and a heavy, sloping roof. Their silence was for my trembling voice, the uncertain expression on my face. It lasted a few seconds, and then someone had the mercy to begin packing his bag to leave, the clock only moments away from summoning us all to lunch.

"Well, off you go," I said to the class, brushing off the entire sequence of events and my own, seemingly childlike poem.

"Love poem's due next week Wednesday. Take your time, let it breathe." The dust of the super-real, its mineral flakes and crystals which had entered on the wings of my poem, began to rise from the debris of the collision. They began to lift into the air and spin in the sunlight filtering down through the windows.

"Journal Collection Number Four on Friday. Good luck!" And with that, I felt safe again. I had reversed the alchemy I had created when I opened myself in this way. But words, once released, cannot be taken back. Mine sat uneasily with Lydia now, and I knew she would not let me off the hook. When the class had nearly emptied out, and I stood straightening my things, packing my bag, only Lydia remained. Her gaze was on the floor now, her lips still moving with silent words. She looked a little perplexed. A little pale.

I folded the poem now, tucked it gently back in to the pages of my journal. Lydia was before me, and Grace lingered in the doorway, waiting for her best friend. The discs of Lydia's eyes seemed to be sounding my soul, and I looked instead at her eyebrows, knitted together now in a tiny frown.

"What's up, Lydia? You okay?"

"Yeah, I just...Well, I feel like I've heard that poem before," she said shyly. The question was in her expression.

"Not possible," I said dismissively. "I wrote it as a kid. Haven't shown it to anyone in years. Must remind you of something," I suggested. A little shadow passed over my consciousness just then; momentarily, there was snow inside my ribcage, a shifting of the light in my head.

"Yeah," she said uncertainly, "I guess so. It's just so familiar." She stood for a moment, like she might speak again, but I was two steps toward the door. I was happy to turn away from shadows and interior snow; I had done it for years and stayed safe in my Hawaiian paradise. I was steady. I *was* the island, especially when one of my students was watching, even if she happened to be a hauntingly familiar Greek beauty. Besides, I'd had my quota of self-revelation for the week and wished to skip into the next emotional state. Lunch sounded good: a noisy cafeteria, a tray sectioned out to serve as a large, no-nonsense plate. Grace, too, gestured for Lydia to come on.

"How's the sestina coming?" I asked, interrupting her thoughts and diverting the conversation successfully as I pulled my keys from my bag.

"It's coming. It's a difficult form—but I love it." Her words gave me pause, and I stopped again. A discussion of formal poetry was perhaps the only thing that might have slowed my momentum toward pizza and the welcome distraction of the dining hall just then. I was a fool for formal structures in verse.

"Yeah?" I said.

"I love how it pushes me, makes me change directions and see what I didn't know I wanted to say," she said thoughtfully. Again, her words took me by surprise, and I was struck by her obvious sense of the form, her simple but astute observation.

"Yes," I said, "and it provides a container. For things

that might otherwise spill across the page. Things that might be too messy without it," I added.

"Yes!" she continued, a little excitement lifting her tone out of its suppressed quiet. "Hard stuff. Painful stuff. It can be not so messy in a sestina."

I wondered for a moment what so young a girl could possibly have experienced in life to inspire such comprehension, but continued anyway: "Or a sonnet or a villanelle. You have so much to look forward to, Lydia. You are a gifted writer. A real artist. Those are rare, you know."

Grace, still standing in the doorway, rolled her eyes.

"We're going to miss the Recycling Club meeting if we don't hurry," she said impatiently, as much to me as to Lydia.

"Ugh—no, it's Habitat for Humanity today. Mia's going to kill us with all this philanthropy," Lydia said, laughing. Mia was a tall, rather gawky looking girl who completed their unlikely trio. She was fairly militant about her causes, I gathered, and a little bossy, though beloved of them both.

"That's a vocab word, by the way," said Lydia, smiling. Indeed 'philanthropy' was one of our words for the week. Again, Grace rolled her eyes.

"Oh God, I don't know how much more geeking out I can take," she said. "You two are hopeless!" Grace often bordered on the too familiar with me, lapsing at times into treating me like a wayward child. I let it go, because she seriously ran the literary magazine that was my responsibility and controlled the entire submission and selection process, as well as the layout.

But Lydia had become dreamy-eyed again and was slightly resisting Grace's tugging at her arm. I had managed by now to lock the classroom door from the inside and herd the two girls onto the lanai that spanned the length of the English building.

"Your poem," Lydia said, pausing again. "It's so sad. Urgent."

It was the precision of her observations that surprised me. I was still flipping through my mental Rolodex of scholarships available to students who show great promise in the literary arts, when Grace slapped me hard on the back with the flat of her hand.

"See ya' Mr. Jameson," she said over her shoulder, practically dragging Lydia in the direction of the dining hall.

"See you, girls," I called after them absently, moving easily on to the next thought: pizza to go and thirty photocopies of "The World is Too Much With Us" by Wordsworth.

I ran into a couple of colleagues on the way to the dining hall and struck up an intense conversation about the upcoming March Madness. The energy with which we approached such discussions was twofold: it had to do with the strong convictions we inevitably held about the various college teams and conferences, but also, and perhaps even more so, with the exhilaration contained in our associations with the NCAA tournament. Its advent each year meant much more to those of us who lived in Hawai'i and its virtual absence of seasons. In other parts of the world, the seasons are vastly indicated by changes in nature. The passage of time and cyclical transition of life is signaled outwardly in and texture and, in particular, by the shape the water takes. In Hawai'i, the water is perennially warm and heavy; it falls from the sky in enormous drops year-round, and it holds the islands in a consistent, if tidal, embrace. Only the very trained eye might perceive evidence of the seasons here, like the way the summer is the "wet season" in South Kona, or how it is always the spring that stirs up Kamakani, the native wind strong enough to tear trees from their roots along the hills of Waimea.

For those of us less attuned, it was clearly ESPN that indicated the seasonal shifts, and March Madness held out to us the promise, every year, of the upcoming summer hustle. The devising of plans for summer travel was just getting underway by the time we were down to the teams allocated to the "Sweet Sixteen," and by the time the "Final Four" had emerged from the college basketball fray, reservations had been made and courses set for places like Tahiti and Indonesia. Not to mention that those faculty vacancies had begun to be filled and the fantasies of incoming teaching recruits were already populating the intoxicating dreams of the young singles among us.

I walked toward the dining hall engaged in these discussions with a couple of math teachers/wrestling coaches, and I nearly forgot the exchanges I had only just had with Lydia and Grace. I forgot the strangeness of what had been felt but not spoken in the moments I chose, inexplicably, to open myself to my students by sharing my poem and turned instead to sports banter. Like that, experience is absorbed into experience. Like that. Like that.

Twelve

Jake

Mia was of Norwegian descent and when she grew into her body one day, she would probably be called statuesque. In the meantime, she was a bit gangly, her white-blond, flyaway hair forming a little halo around her face. Her eyes were bright blue and appeared to always contain a secret, flitting behind them like a small bird. Sauntering across the lawn with Grace and Lydia, she looked like a tall, pale bird herself, between two smaller, darker avian varieties. I stood watching them out the window as the light of the Xerox machine passed again and again beneath my hand, producing copy after copy of contemporary poetry handouts. Lydia had a streak of purple in her black hair that day, and a long purple skirt wound itself around her legs as she walked. It gave her the appearance of an inverted, black-stemmed flower, closing in on itself the way a hibiscus does when the sun disappears. Grace was barefooted, as usual, her rubber slippers dangling from her right hand, her left arm hooked with Mia's right, as they walked toward the faculty workroom.

I observed the three of them as one replays a dream. They were an *already memory;* I saw them as actually gone, and these the apparitions of something I used to know. Used to *be,* even. They were a mirage moving undulantly toward me, under a straining sun and the fleeting shadows of distant flags. Soundlessly and as if underwater. Under the impress of time. I was mesmerized by the mingling of past and present. The super-real and the real, which I had felt pretty confident to have severed successfully after my unexpected little foray into their union, mingled here unapologetically. There they were as one, time a non-entity. *I saw Kenya between Sam and Athena.* They smiled and laughed as they moved across the grass.

I stood there at the copy machine with my travel mug full of lukewarm coffee. Anticipating their arrival, I swung toward the door of the workroom to meet their intent faces. They had come specifically for me, and I stood there, more or less frozen, their figures outlined by sunlight in the doorway. I was a little breathless.

"Mr. Jameson," Grace said with some urgency, "I can't make the Lit Mag meeting this afternoon." The substantive and regular nature of her words drew me out of my reverie, called me back to the space we now occupied. I faltered, perhaps imperceptibly, and then transitioned seamlessly from illusion to reality. Just like that. I turned back to my copying.

"Family emergency?" I said, my voice tinged with sarcasm.

"No…"

"Doctor's appointment?" I suggested, resetting the machine for two-sided copies of "Talk the Big Hand Down" by Victoria Redel.

"Not exactly," Grace said. I could see her in my mind's eye, shifting her weight from bare foot to bare foot in the doorway, but I didn't turn to face her right away. When I finally did, I saw that she was looking sheepish, her cohorts smiling rather obsequiously.

"Grace, you are so predictable. Don't you think I know Kawaihae Harbor is four foot and glassy this afternoon?" Mia and Lydia giggled and looked to Grace for a response. She seemed miffed.

"Come on, Mr. Jameson. You know I'm only doing Lit Mag for the service credit. We all know that Lydia is the real poet…" said Grace, as if this last comment was relevant in any way. Lydia blushed, and Mia nudged her so hard she almost crashed into the faculty mailboxes.

"I think after three years of Lit Mag staff, your service hours are complete, yeah?" I said to Grace unmercifully. She looked embarrassed in front of her friends and I almost regretted saying that.

"Anyway," I continued, "you don't have to be a gifted poet to be able to lay out a page for the school's literary magazine. Plus, I need you for the web version. You're the only one who knows the application."

Grace looked a little desperate. "Look, if you let me out of the meeting today, I'll lay out the whole thing next week…and I'll get Lydia to submit a poem." The look she flashed at Lydia contained in it both an apology and a silent plea.

"Grace!" Lydia squealed. I was interested, though, and turned my attention to Lydia.

"I have always wished you would submit some of your stuff," I told her. "What your write for my class is really, very good."

"Please, Lydia," Grace whined. "69's is cranking today. I'll seriously owe you."

Lydia looked at her dubiously, her mouth drawn a little to the side. "You already do owe me," she muttered.

"Right, don't remind me," said Grace.

"Nah, you don't have to, Lydia," I said, wanting to release her from Grace's ridiculous 'deal.'

"But Grace," I said, "I expect to see you at the computer next week." My voice was stern, but I could feel myself smiling a little. I was a sucker for surf and knew that I would be out in the lineup for glass-off, too, just as soon as I could dismiss the meeting.

"Done. Thanks, Mr. Jameson. You 'da bessss!" she said in her best mock pidgin. Taking Lydia's face in her hand, and squeezing her cheeks until Lydia looked like a fish, she said "Mwaaaa!" Then, without warning, she swung around and, hopping the railing of the lanai, jogged off down the grassy hill below us. Peering after her, we could see a car idling in the lot, piled high with surfboards and kids. Grace threw them the hang loose sign on her way down, indicating the success of her little venture.

"Let's go, Lydia," said Mia, changing gears suddenly. She was tugging on the strap of Lydia's bag and already heading out the door.

"Recycling Club," said Lydia in explanation, "She's the president." Before I knew it they were both out the door and around the corner. I heard Mia call to me from outside through the wood slat windows of the faculty room.

"See you Monday, Mr. Jameson!" she said, and they were gone.

I didn't give much thought to my little lapse into memory-reality. It wasn't entirely out of the ordinary, though such mingling of the super-real and the real didn't normally involve other living people. I would have to write about it, I thought, and returned to my Xeroxing.

That night, however, I dragged two rolled up canvases from the corner next to my dresser. I sat down on my couch with a beer and slowly untied the violet ribbon that bound them, let them roll open of their own accord to reveal Athena's numinous figure, her acrylic goodbye. "Departure," she had called it, and I had trembled at the implications of this title for years. Now it seemed oddly normal, the apparent anachronism of such nomenclature, its apparent presaging of events, no longer surprising at all. It was as if I had rolled up past, present and future in that bundle of paintings and unfurled here before me, they commingled un-extravagantly and without fanfare.

I took a swig of my beer and sat back, breathing deeply the Waimea night air. Something familiar stirred in me, though it could no longer be called pain or suffering. Just a sort of mild sorrow or half-remembered sense of something lost or misplaced somehow. I hadn't looked at these paintings for years; they were so much a part of my sensibility that they stirred no new feeling, dug up no new emotion that I could identify. I enjoyed the sensation of the beer in my belly as it turned warm there and without thinking picked up the telephone.

I had to dial 411 to get Angela's number. I knew she was still in Berkeley, teaching now at the university. Last I had heard she was engaged to Brock and was probably married by now. When the line connected, it was Angela's voice.

"Hi there, you have reached Dr. Angela Wilder." She had kept her name, I remember thinking. "I'm not in right now, but feel free to leave me a message. Or, you can try me in my office on the main university number, extension 3557. Take care, and I'll get back to you as soon as I can." There was a smile in her tone.

After the beep I left some ridiculous message about calling from Hawai'i, having heard she was engaged some years ago, wondering if she still surfed. Speculating that she was probably married or had kids by now.

"Number's the same," I said, but as I started to leave it, the voicemail interrupted me with a beep. "Nice," I said and hung up. A little disgusted with myself for no real reason, I picked up my keys and headed for the door. Something in me felt unsettled, and I knew it had something to do with the day's events. With my sharing of my writing, the mirage on the lawn, Lydia's probing questions, her comments about my poem.

As I pulled into town, it began to rain softly—*typical Waimea weather,* I remember thinking. I pulled into the Waimea Java lot for maybe the thousandth time over the past several years, and got out of the car. The coffee shop closed at three every day, but I wasn't there for that. I stood on the lawn enclosed on three sides by the Paniolo Square and faced the darkened windows above Waimea Java, a fine mist dampening my face. I knew Phyllis lived there, and a bare bulb illuminated her sign, as always: "Clairvoyant Healings and Readings."

Over the years I had known her to have a small but steady clientele of New-Agey types, who came and went regularly, their footfalls on the stairs always audible from the coffee shop below. I had had many interesting and philosophical discussions with Phyllis over tea and coffee on the occasions she had chosen to sit down at my table and chat. She and I were an unlikely pair, but I enjoyed her company immensely. I generally avoided talking to her about her 'work,' perhaps out of some remote fear I might lose respect for a woman I considered to be quite grounded, despite her vague claims to otherworldly vision.

That night I stood there contemplating those claims and their inherent promises, collecting the rain in my hair, my hands shoved in the pockets of my jeans. I couldn't have said what led me to Phyllis, or to her yard, as it were, since I never actually approached her door. Eventually the chill drew me out of my cloudy contemplation and I headed back to my car and my Kamalani Dorm apartment. For a while, I didn't think again about my visit to Phyllis'. I had learned not to think too hard about things I had already done in my life. The past swirled around my ears like a natural fog, but my own actions I chose not to scrutinize.

Standing in front of Phyllis' house (and Waimea Java) in the rain and the dark was not the craziest thing I'd done. There was something I meant to learn, perhaps by speaking with Phyllis. Some question that was forming in my head, or even my heart, but which had yet to take the shape of language. There was a thing that Phyllis knew, I thought, though what that thing was I could not have named.

I saw Phyllis soon after I stood beneath her window in the rain. She asked me if I hadn't wanted to pay her a visit in her 'office,' eyeing me carefully; I remember thinking for a moment that she might feel my head for fever. After she let me go on for several minutes about how she really might be clairvoyant, she admitted to having seen me that night, standing there in the dark. She suggested that I come back during "regular business hours" to ask her my questions.

"About angels," I had whispered to her, looking over

my shoulder to make sure I wasn't overheard and feeling completely idiotic. She had smiled knowingly and given me her characteristic wink, but I had yet to turn up at her place. I felt resistant and could admit to myself that there was a little bit of fear around the whole thing for me. It didn't help that Phyllis fit perfectly the stereotype for the old gypsy woman who reads a crystal ball and tells you the precise date and means of your death before you can object.

When Lydia finally shared a poem in workshop, it was the one spawned by my prompt for 'an unconventional love poem' in the previous semester. A few months had passed since the day I assigned it as a journal entry, and she had taken the opportunity to craft the thing and to prepare it for her final portfolio. Already March, enough time had passed for her to take it through many drafts…and never involve me in the process. I tried not to take it personally. When she read the poem aloud, her steady gaze moving slowly between the faces of her audience and the page, I was floored. It was not only the precision of her language and the evocativeness of her images, but also the way I felt myself respond to it. It felt familiar to me, as if I had heard it before, and yet I knew it to be new in my experience.

She stood before the class in her purple hoodie with the sleeves pulled down over her hands; she had cut holes into the wristbands to admit her thumbs to the outside world. By now we all knew her favorite to be purple and expected at least one aspect of her clothing to bear some shade or other of the royal hue. That day, she wore several very tiny little braids originating around the crown of her head and ending in miniscule, purple rubber bands she had probably coaxed from someone with braces. They gave her the appearance of a little girl, though the words she uttered seemed alarmingly adult.

"In the silver silence you press your face against me,"

she began. The sibilance of the line and the warm tones of her voice entranced more than one of the males in the room. Still, her expression was open, innocent as she continued: "and breathe your love into my melon skin, crawl inside the space/ I have made for you here. If I could give words to this movement/ along my spine, this careless wind around my ears as I imagine you,/ I would not have to dream, but only make the truth real, give it weight/ and place it in your palm: gift of sweetest intent."

In an instant, Angela's Tara figurine crossed my consciousness, my own words about the *real* trailing behind it like a zephyr. I saw Athena's hand trailing behind *her* in her "Departure." I felt my stomach broaden, flatten and then slowly and uncomfortably return to its right shape. I felt aroused, I must admit, but not by the timid figure of Lydia standing before the class, now innocently looking to me for her next cue. I was attracted to the poem. To the space it created. If I could have climbed into that space, I think I would have.

Instead, I was called back to the present by the delayed applause of the students. They were clearly expressing their appreciation for what Lydia had crafted and unselfconsciously shared. In my own innocence, and limited understanding, I felt slightly ashamed. I quickly guided the students in a session of commentary on Lydia's poem, avoiding my own reaction to it.

When class was over, I was left with Lydia and Grace, Grace again framed by the door and obviously eager to go. I must have been staring at Lydia, perhaps contemplating what I might say to her regarding her work, because Grace said, "She's good, huh."

"Yeah," I said, "she's good." They were all the words I could muster at the moment. Lydia allowed herself a small smile, looking down at her shoes. Unlike most of her peers who donned rubber slippers or leather sandals, Lydia was wearing her characteristic black and white "Mary Janes" with the faces of cats on the toes.

"She has a million of them," Grace continued, still talking about Lydia's poems. "She says she doesn't even know where they come from. It's weird. She's like Shelley or Keats, you know…how they had to, like, drop everything and write things down sometimes. That's Lydia. Loopy," she added, twirling her forefinger around at her temple in the familiar gesture for insanity.

"Hello, I'm right here!" said Lydia, embarrassed and a little disconcerted. I ignored them both in this regard.

"I'm curious, Lydia…" I began, not knowing where I would go with this opening.

"Yeah, don't worry," Lydia interrupted. "I'm not having sex. Just imagining it." Her assumption about my concern and my question threw me off, and I cleared my throat in discomfort.

"Okay. That's not really what I was wondering, but…good to know." I loved her frankness. Her genuineness. She felt familiar to me, and in the past weeks I had had to consciously check my behavior toward her. She was in fact *not* familiar to me, nor *could* she be under the circumstances. Even my attention to her poetry sometimes felt too intense.

"That's some imagination," I added, fairly lost in my own thought at that point. Lydia laughed at me, and I saw that she was totally at ease. It startled me how comfortable she could be in my presence, the natural shroud that normally separates student from teacher undetectable with her. Usually there was some mythical sensibility that surrounded a beloved teacher, some fluid but impassable boundary that students knew to respect and could trust to be respected by their teachers without exception. It's what made it safe for girls to flirt with their male teachers; they were trying on their wiles but knew, indeed depended on the fact that, their attentions would not be returned.

Pretty girls made a game of it; I knew the game well enough. It had been somewhat less pronounced in the past few years, as I had become older, replaced perhaps by younger, newer teachers in the school. But there was always some girl student or other who wanted to see if she could make you squirm. I had become a master at diffusing such situations, sending a girl on her way firmly but without crushing her self-esteem. It was what they wanted, I felt. They were still children, though they occupied often disconcertingly adult bodies, and like all children they wanted the adults in their lives to set limits.

Lydia surprised me again by switching the subject: "Hey, do we really have to wait for graduation to have a beer with you? Mia and Grace and I want to treat our favorite English teacher." Grace perked up now, but I was impenetrable.

"Graduation. If even then!" I shook my head and shooed them toward the door. The students in my next class were already filing in.

"Hey, too bad," said Grace. "Our birthdays are coming up."

"What?" I said, taken aback.

"Yeah, April sixteenth. We'll be eighteen. Me and Grace and Mia. We were all born within twenty-four hours of each other. Technically, Grace was born on the seventeenth, but we always celebrate together on the sixteenth." Her innocence was crushing. Without quite processing why, I felt as if a liter of acid had just been dumped into my stomach.

"That's crazy," I finally said.

"Not that crazy," said Grace. "See you later, Mr. Jameson." And with that they both picked up their things and trotted off to their next classes.

Thirteen

Jake

Walking home to my apartment that day after class, my head was full of thoughts about angels, rebirth, the possibilities around that whole cycle. *What if it was possible to meet up with the same spirit…twice in a life time?* No, I thought, but I didn't fully dismiss the idea; nor did I dismiss the mild alarm that was occupying my belly. It was too great a coincidence that these three girls shared the same birthday as Kenya, Sam and Athena. It was too bizarre, too dizzying, to think about.

I saw, as I drew parallel with the dorm, that there was a woman standing on my lanai, her long, brown hair swaying slightly in the afternoon breeze. She was leaning on the railing and looking out over the landscape. There was, at her feet, what looked like a large backpack and a surfboard bag. I was intrigued and picked up my pace as I walked. Two or three boys made little whistling sounds as I went by them, all of them having noticed her there; used to their running commentary on my life, I ignored them. As I got nearer, I saw that it was Angela, and her easy smile greeted me.

"Nice view you have here!" she called to me, grinning.

"Whoah, hey! Angela!"

"Hope you don't mind me showing up like this. I'm passing through," she explained.

"Passing through?" I said, joining her on the lanai. "An island?" I teased. We hugged a little awkwardly, but she felt good in my arms. Her little brush of a kiss on my cheek reminded me of Pleasure Point, of the maple trees lining the quad at Lighthouse High, of saltwater taffy. She was perhaps all that remained of my youth, and I had missed her.

"I'm on my way to New Zealand," she said. "My aunt has a B&B down there in Raglan. I'm going to spend some time with her. Anyway, you had left that message, and..."

"You didn't call back," I said, almost concealing the tiny seed of bitterness under my tongue. I had reached out to her. It was my first attempt. Delayed, yes, but made in earnest. My pride had been hurt, and almost two months had passed since then.

"Yeah. Sorry about that."

"Everything okay? I mean—well, come in," I offered, recovering my wits and my manners.

"Yeah, I, uh, didn't get married."

"So I gathered," I said, shaking her empty ring finger playfully. "Want a beer?"

"I'd love one." While I took two Fire Rock Pale Ales out of the fridge and opened them, Angela moved around the room slowly. She was observing all of my little trinkets and shedding the outer layers of clothing she had worn on the air-conditioned trip from San Francisco to my door. Finally: a pale grey camisole that clung to her lean, fit body as she moved about my living room. I thought of the boys watching her arrive with her backpack and surfboard. I hoped they hadn't spoken to her; they could say the most ridiculous things.

I handed Angela her beer and turned to face the wall she was perusing. It was the one that held the framed reproduction of Chagall's "The Walk," and she looked at me now a little quizzically. Nearly eighteen years had passed since she gave me this image. It was on the card she'd bought in the Capitola Mercantile on a June morning in 1989:

The fog was just lifting off the esplanade, and the sun was casting a yellowish hue on the little row of buildings there, on the sheen of the sea undulating beyond them. Angela had a neatly stitched wound on her forehead, and her mother was nearby—had not let her out of her sight for weeks. This mother knew now how quickly one's happiness could be undone. She pretended to peruse the ceramic cups and dishes one aisle over, but was every minute conscious of her beautiful, fragile girl, slowly turning the display rack of greeting cards.

But of course I invent this image, because I was miles away at the time. Miles away.

I looked at the painting with her now, my sleeve brushing her bare arm at my side. Here is what I saw: The figure below— *I am the man in the suit,* Angela had written in her card, (*see my sad little smile*)— his feet were rooted to the earth. His smile *was* a little sad, but it was something you could count on. There was nothing hidden beneath it. That was clear. *And you are the woman in pink,* she had written. *She thought of me as floating, too,* I remember thinking rather incredulously. I reflected that I often thought of myself as floating, out in the atmosphere somewhere. In orbit around the planet of self. The atoms were falling differently these days, though, making a different pattern on the unkempt ground. I felt expansive at times, and at other times…fearful.

The moment passed, and Angela did not ask me to explain myself or verbally make the link between her gift and the painting so prominently displayed in my living room. I loved that about her, too. She seemed never to require words. I was all about language. Of words, I had written, *They are all, they are all,* and I meant it—but moments like these suggested that secretly, they might be nothing, these words I so hoarded, pressed to my chest, released lovingly, even jealously, like little birds or butterflies. I was trying to figure out whether or not that terrified me, when she started laughing. A soft little tumble of air and voice that was her familiar giggle. So much was surprisingly familiar, and I remember thinking about that. How shared experience can link two people in a way it might take lifetimes to connect with another.

I checked my thoughts, knowing she was reading my mind again. With Angela, I had begun to notice, I felt like I had a flip-top head—like all its contents lay bare to her, with or without my consent. And then her touch: just her hand on my arm, and a little herding motion to which I happily succumbed, so that in an instant we had moved onto the balcony and were chatting gregariously about every topic under the lazily setting sun.

She asked me about life as a teacher at H.I.A. About marine mammals who included Hawai'i in their circuit between Mexico and Alaska. About Hawaiian culture and language. She was curious about everything, and I was happy to share the little knowledge I had gathered in my years on the island. She had left her post at Berkeley and delegated all of her therapy clients to other capable psychologists. Now she was having a delayed little walkabout, she said, just finding her way outside of the "masculine paradigm of success." She had left Brock, she told me, almost at the last minute. Not at the altar but perhaps as horribly. At night and in the rain—with screaming.

"After a ten year courtship, I finally say yes, and then…it seems I'm having a little trouble moving forward. The past has such—I don't know, it's like the idea of the shadow past," she said.

"How what didn't happen is as important as what actually did?" I suggested, knowing exactly to which book she referred.

"Yeah," she said, and began quoting the Olga Broumas poem I loved: "What hasn't happened intrudes, so much/ Hasn't yet happened." It was a poem I had always used to teach the importance of punctuation and line break—how with careful placement they can create fluidity of meaning, raise questions about intent.

I couldn't help but continue the recitation: "…the gutting/ loneliness/ of the present where/ what hasn't happened will/ not be ignored, intrudes, separates/ from the conversation…"

"…like milk/ from cream," she finished. I took her

chin in my hand for a moment, smiling at her beautifully mature face. The woman from the girl. Here. In my hand.

"You okay?" I asked.

"I will be," she said, and removed my hand from her chin tenderly. She was not interested in being babied. We talked all evening and into the night. Our conversation took us across decades and continents and led us easily into the realms of philosophy and literature. We laughed, too, about not "feeling" thirty-five and in her case, not looking it.

"You're not doing too bad there yourself, champ. How is it that you're still single?" she said airily, tipping her beer in my direction.

"You know—the Big Island isn't exactly the hot spot for meeting women." I was borrowing the old excuse. I had dated several women over the years and kept them all safely at arm's length until they in turn became frustrated and impatient and moved on. It was a cycle familiar to me by then. "It's pretty quiet here. I work a lot…" I continued.

"Oh, you didn't really have to answer that," she said, apologetically.

"I know," I said simply, but inwardly I wondered why I was babbling.

"You still surfing a lot?" she asked. *Bless her for changing subjects,* I remember thinking.

"Yeah, well, then there's that. The real love of my life."

"Ah," she said, "the truth comes out. You're having an affair with the sea. That bitch!"

We both laughed and turned our gazes toward the horizon, now darkening as it had that first night I spent in Kamalani Dormitory and had spoken to Angela on the phone. It was hard to believe that so much time had passed. Something about the combination of three beers and the blood orange hue of the sky, or maybe it was having Angela there, who was one of the only people who knew everything—about that time. It gave me a sort of confidence within subjects I might have otherwise avoided. I rushed headlong into the conversation that had been dominating my thoughts all that day and perhaps for weeks preceding it. It was a conversation I had been having with myself, and I lunged now toward the relief of having someone with whom I could share it. I completely disregarded how it might be received by the present company. She *was* my Tara, after all, wasn't she?

"I've been having some weird thoughts lately," I said to her confessionally.

"Yeah," she said jokingly, "Me too!" She giggled again, but I held steady.

"No," I said, "I mean it. Like…" I noticed how attentively Angela was now looking at me. Her eyes were moist, expectant.

"Athena is still on my mind. More so in the last couple of years," I began. I suppose Angela was a little disappointed with this opening, but if she was I didn't see it.

"I've had to come up with a few theories, you know, to reconcile myself to things like that. Incongruencies with my ideas about God and the world," I continued. "It's like, my whole belief system got shot out of a cannon that night on the lake." My old metaphor. "For a long time I thought it was irrecoverable, but then…then I realized I would have to put it back together again. Differently. Some of the pieces are the same, but I've become open to a lot more. My closed system didn't give me a very satisfying answer to all those why's." I wanted to talk about life and death and the concept of the hereafter; Angela could not have seen this as the intimate thing that it was. For her, I was making the same choice I always made. Past over present. The super-real over the real. Floating in the sky, maintaining my distant orbit, never standing on the soil—there, next to her.

"I think I know what you mean," she finally said, and I didn't doubt it. The flip-top head thing again. She could read my thoughts, it seemed. And more, she seemed to understand them—without judgment. Talking to her now was like a healing balm, I remember thinking, never considering what it was like for her. You would think the years would have taught me to be less egocentric, but they had not. She continued:

"Like when people ask me what my faith is, I have to say something like, I'm eclectic."

"Yeah," I agreed, "I bet that gets a mixed response."

"At best."

"Well, I have this idea about people who die young. They're always the best ones, you know?"

"Yeah," she said, looking a little forlorn.

"And it's always the ones who were brightest, happiest, gave the most of themselves to others." I was gaining momentum now, wearing the little blinders of self-indulgence.

"Hence the song," she added, but the irony in her eyes was lost on me.

"Right!" I was encouraged by her apparent agreement. "*Only the Good Die Young,*" I quoted.

"Mmmmm," she breathed.

"Well," I ventured, "I think they're angels." This from a pseudo-intellectual high school English teacher, I thought. Impressive. But it was out. I'd said it. It was a relief.

"What?"

"Yeah," I said, still holding my breath a little. I eyed her cautiously before continuing, but she was unreadable, that *sad little smile* playing on her lips. "I think they're angels. Mrs. Gates said something to me when she showed me Athena's paintings. That day of the service."

"Yeah?" Angela's tone was gentle, tentative.

"She said, 'She was not long for this earth.' I've thought about that. A lot. You know, she's right. Athena was not long for this earth. She was too light, too bright. Sam and Kenya, too," I finished.

"Three angels," Angela intoned.

"Yeah!" I exclaimed, imagining that she agreed with me completely. She stood up then and began to clear some of the dishes. Suddenly, there was a new tension and something seemed to have ended; I wondered if it was just our discussion. I felt somewhat like a little boy who knows something has gone terribly wrong but can't begin to imagine what.

"Jake," she finally said, having stacked all the plates and serving dishes. "I like your idea. It's sweet. Beautiful, even. But…"

"But what? Lately it's like Athena is right here. I feel her very near me." I couldn't talk about Lydia, but I flirted with that disaster now. For Angela, the dam broke.

"You know, Jake. I'm not sure it's entirely healthy for you to be obsessing about a dead girl nearly twenty years after her death." A new and not entirely benign light was in her eyes. Her voice was edgy. I was immediately defensive, and we both knew that all the wrong words had been said but couldn't follow the thread back to the first wrong syllable. What did it matter anyway, I remember thinking.

"Obsessing, huh?" I said angrily.

"Well, Jake, come on. You're thirty-five years old. She's still eighteen. She always will be. And she's perfect. It's like you said: 'How can you compete with that?' How can you compete with someone who has been immortalized? Someone who is incapable of making a mistake because she no longer moves in the flesh!" Her voice had reached quite a pitch, and her eyes were full of tears. For a split second I caught a glimpse of all the ways I had been a disappointment to Angela.

"I'm sorry, Angela," I said, reaching for her rigid shoulder. She moved back almost imperceptibly, inwardly recoiling from my touch. "I just…"

"I know," she interrupted. Her voice had become gentle again, if a little regretful. We cleaned the kitchen in silence, neither of us having the heart to drink any more or try to spark up a new conversation.

I lay awake that night on my living room couch for a long while. I was sifting through my past experience and trying to figure out how it translated into what I had just said to Angela. What was I saying, after all? What belief, or hope, was behind those words? I felt foolish, but I also had to admit that I meant what I said. I had become increasingly curious about reincarnation. I remembered that I had once met a Waimea lady who was certain that her son was the reincarnated soul of her late brother-in-law. She had named the baby after his uncle, which had served to perpetuate the perceived likeness. When the boy had come through my class at H.I.A., he had struck me as one of those souls—just a little too light. A little too bright. Athlete, scholar, empath.

But the boy had passed through H.I.A. without event and had even graduated with s from Chaminade University. I believed he was now in med school somewhere on the East Coast. Maybe he would make it, I thought; he'd managed to fool the gods thus far, to sneak past the destructive forces of Pele, our Hawaiian version of Shiva the Destroyer. I fell asleep with my head full of the theological and philosophical soup that was my belief system. With the sound of Angela's light breathing just reaching me from the next room, I slept a thick, dreamless night and woke to the smell of coffee.

PART THREE

Spring 2007

Fourteen

Angela

Standing on Jake's balcony at the school, I felt a little foolish. I had turned up, unannounced, to this: his life, of which I knew almost nothing, and his home, to which I had not been officially invited. Twelve years had passed since our last face-to-face encounter, also on a balcony, and all I had for an indication that I might be welcome now was half a voicemail left almost two months before in a familiar tone.

I had left Brock a year ago, almost to the date. My parents' dreams of a big wedding and imminent grandparenthood had disintegrated, along with a hundred and fifty wedding invitations, which Brock threw out into the street during a rainstorm and our last fantastic fight. He had driven away recklessly, like a boy, his tires skidding wildly under the sleek body of his sports car. I had stood in the rain, still holding the lid of the box that had housed the invitations, in alphabetical order, feeling an alchemical mixture of despair and liberation.

I remember the next morning having seen bits of pale parchment with our names and intentions bleeding into gutter water. By then I was tired of crying and had cleaned up the mess with a dust pan and bucket, ignoring my s, who must certainly have been privy to the previous night's scene. Brock had been perfect, as far as everyone else in my life was concerned, and I knew they pitied me as they carted their children off to school, their travel mugs neatly fitted into the cup holders of their sedans and SUVs.

I had spent the past year trying to recoup; I continued living in the Sausalito home Brock and I had rented together, commuting three days a week to the university and back, but it had been no use. I had become successful in every way that society measures success, and I still felt that there was more to be, more to know.

I had an aunt who lived in Raglan, New Zealand and ran a guesthouse out at Whale Bay. It was mostly surfers who frequented her three-storey, oceanfront abode, and she fed them delicious meat pies and local greens in between their mind-blowing surf sessions in the bay. At night they curled up in little down nests in her various guest rooms and dreamed of the next day's waves and pies. It sounded perfect to me.

I had wanted to go there for years, and it seemed a good time, now that my old life seemed fairly irrecoverable and my new one completely inconceivable. I was heading there now, with a single backpack and my tail pretty much between my legs. I had taken care of business before I left; no tragic rearrangement of my life plans could alter my responsible demeanor. Still, I felt like I'd cut myself loose and was now unmoored, out at sea, not so much floating as diving down. If one held the globe and marked the spot where I had just come from, as well as the spot I was headed, they would see that they are directly opposite one another. *Perhaps I should have dug my way to New Zealand,* I remember having thought. *Would've been cheaper.*

The fact was, I didn't know when I'd be back. I knew I could get a work permit in New Zealand; I was a skilled migrant in a field where there was a shortage, and my aunt had offered to keep me for as long as I wished. Hawai'i and Jake were in the direct path of my voyage, so I had stopped over for a few days. If there was something between us, besides three very lovely ghosts, I wanted to know.

When I saw Jake walking along the path in front of the dormitory, I saw that he hadn't changed. It was easy to admit now that I was in love with him and maybe always had been; but it was also easy to categorize that feeling as among those never to be consummated and better left hidden in the recesses of my secret self. It was a familiar process from leap of heart to containment of feeling, and I underwent it now without flinching, so that when he got close enough to recognize me, I was able to give him an easy smile that was the real expression of my happiness to see him. No more and no less. Of self-discipline I knew a thing or two, but God he was beautiful.

His floppy hair was like it had been when he was a boy, but now it was down to his broad shoulders. Instead of swimming, surfing now maintained the tapered "v" of his torso, and his skin was brown, finely wrinkled at the edges of his eyes. Evidence of smiling, I thought, and squinting in the bright equatorial sun. He had a messenger's bag slung across his body, and he was straining to make out my identity. The sun behind him now, his body was dressed in light; his familiar gait had in it a little bounce, a little swing.

The awkwardness of our initial meeting melted quickly away, as did the afternoon, under the influence of several Hawaiian beers and a string of appetizers Jake called "pupus." I had wanted to take it all in, had felt that it might be the last time I saw Jake and this funny little apartment, now full of the relics of his life in Hawai'i and traveling abroad. I wanted him, to be sure, and some part of me considered trying to seduce him. I saw him more than once regarding my skin, my hair, holding my gaze for a moment too long now and then over the course of the evening. Perhaps that was all there was to do: create the physical explosion that would forever ground us, shatter our old relationship to one another. We would be lovers for one night, and I could catch a plane in the morning.

But I knew better than that. I had learned to be braver than this, less self-indulgent. If our connections to people were to remain real, we couldn't abuse them under the excesses of pleasure. All temporary hiatuses from the actual, from what we know to be real, lead us back to where we started. I knew to revere the real. I knew that Jake did, too. Love seemed to have taken a preeminent place in my psyche. It was love that circumscribed my actions that night. Love I had carried in my heart for Jake for nearly eighteen years now; love I still bore our mutual friends who were no more.

At some point he began talking nonsense, or so it seemed to me. He wanted to talk about Athena. He said things about angels and blame, theory and faith, spirit and flesh. He said he felt Athena near; this was right about the time I lost it. I said what I meant, though I think it hurt him. I said what I had wanted to say on the balcony after our college graduation. I essentially accused him of loving the dead more than the living. The years had given me courage, or at least abandon. How he did not hear my absolute love for him as I spoke, I do not know.

I felt so lonely as we washed the dishes together, cleared away the evidence of our careful pleasure. I went to bed that night resolved to leave in the morning. I would go while Jake was at school. Leave a note and a bottle of wine.

Then I woke thinking about the Chagall painting Jake had hung in his living room. "The Walk," which to me had always symbolized my relationship to him. I had given it to him all those years ago, almost before we had even assumed those positions. Wasn't that proof of something? Was it even possible that he had as little understanding now, of its metaphor, as he had then? Inside that painting, I wanted to yank on that hand, pull him violently out of his orbit. Why did he have to dwell in the realm of the holy? Why did he insist on disconnecting himself, lifting off, relying on those of us below to manage the few strings that anchored him to the earth?

I wanted Jake to fill his pockets with stones or tie fishing sinkers into his hair, float gently down to me, so that he might see me eye to eye. Know me for what I was, not how I appeared from such great heights. And yet, I felt the most profound patience with regard to him, too. I had always felt it my job to stand there grinning and hold that hand as he drifted on air. In spite of myself, I knew I would continue to do exactly that.

I felt only compassion as I watched him sleep there on the couch, the morning sun's glow barely seeping into the air above the distant volcano to light the room. I was his Tara. I had sprung from his tears and would help him in his work. It was work that would perhaps never be completed, but my role in it was noble. I would go to New Zealand. Raglan called. But first I would make this beautiful man a cup of coffee and suspend my judgment for a day or two.

Fifteen

Jake

I talked Angela into extending her stay with me for a full week and a half. She could use my Jeep during the days when I was teaching, and then we could go adventuring together after I got off work. I wanted her to see the volcano, the City of Refuge called Pu'u Honua O Honaunau, Pololu Valley, all places I held dear and sent every guest I had had over the years. She could surf all day long if she wished, and when I got off work, she would be there, and we could play.

We stayed up late that second night marking each place on an old road map I had, and she made little notes in a moleskin book, which she wouldn't let me get anywhere near. She felt self-conscious about being a closet poet, and since I was the "real poet," refused to let me read anything she had penned. On her third night on the island, I sent her with a couple of female faculty friends to the Blue Dolphin to hear a local band and eat some fresh seafood. I had the last lit mag meeting of the semester that evening; it was the night of our deadline, and it promised to be a late one.

Mia, Grace and Lydia were all present, as were a handful of other students inclined toward poetry, all of them working to pair student art work meaningfully with student writing for the April edition of *Ka Mele*, which simply means, *The Song*. I had just finished doling out the Waimea Java, which Angela had generously offered to deliver to my apartment before heading down to the Blue Dolphin in my friend Elyse's car.

"Sweet," said Grace. She took the huge cup of hot chocolate from my hand and swung her chair back toward the computer screen that had framed the back of her head for the past two hours. Over her shoulder: "Thanks Mr. Jameson."

"No problem," I said. I often reflected on the parallels between my job as a teacher and that of a waiter at a restaurant.

"Would you like some butter with that?" I would say sarcastically to a student who had raised his hand simply to have me walk over to his desk so he could hand me a paper or ask me a question I had just answered. "Maybe a little garlic?" The kids would look at me quizzically, but it was my little joke to myself, and I found that as I grew older, I cared less and less about having my humour appreciated by those around me. As long as I was entertained, I reasoned. That night, moving around the room with my little cardboard carriers of drinks, the parallel was complete and perhaps less funny than I had found it before. All I needed was a pair of roller skates.

"Wow!" I said, looking over the shoulder of a boy named Koa, who was pairing some particularly dark poetry with some tempestuous-looking oil paintings of the sea at twilight. "Those look terrific!" He was creating a border for the pages that resembled seashells, but when you looked closer, they were faces.

"Almost finished, huh?" I asked Grace from across the room.

"I'd say another hour or two will do it for the web-based stuff," she called back to me without taking her eyes from her work.

"About that for the print version, too," said Mia.

"Excellent. Vat of whipped cream on my desk if you want some. Take a break if you'd like, and we'll crank this thing out before ten."

As everyone began moving and chatting, preparing for the last stretch of the evening, it was Grace who started in about Angela.

"So, Mr. J., I hear there's a hottie staying at your place."

"A hottie, huh?" I said warily, busying myself with my own coffee and the creamer.

"Yeah," chimed Mia, "the guys on your hall say she's really pretty—well, not in those terms, of course. Who is she? Your secret lover?" She and Grace were both smiling smugly.

"No, nothing like that," I answered quickly. "She's a friend. I've actually known her since I was your age."

"What was that, like the 60's? No wait, the Jurassic Period, maybe?" Grace was fond of teasing me about my age.

"Grace!" squealed Lydia, ever respectful of propriety and obviously concerned about my feelings. I thought that was cute, but I had no qualms about being called "old" by teenagers. I distinctly remembered having thought at their age that anyone over twenty-five was 'too old' and certainly past their prime. It came with the territory. In fact, the older I got, the younger fifty sounded to me, though I had years to go before I had to worry about hitting the half-century mark.

"No—it was the eighties. You know, 'Everybody Wang Chung tonight'?" I said, giving my impression of Molly Ringwald's little kicky dance in *The Breakfast Club* and snapping my fingers. It was greeted with silence. I think I actually enjoyed the awkwardness of the moment.

"Right. You don't know. It was a good time. Peg-legged pants, leg warmers. Oh wait—you guys are wearing that stuff, aren't you? Hmmm—what does this mean? Maybe there truly is 'nothing new under the sun'." I was fond of quoting Ecclesiastes in this way, and at least half of them rolled their eyes in response and made their way back to their workspaces.

"Ouch! Geez! Alright, you guys. Back to work. I'd like to get home some time before midnight."

"I bet you would," commented Mia, mischievously

refusing to let the original topic die.

"Mia, you are approaching the line…" It was a comment that she, and especially Grace, heard frequently from me. They both giggled softly and went back to their lit mag work.

It was still bothering me that the girls were getting ready to celebrate their birthdays together. The sixteenth was less than a week away. While I hardly attached any weight to that day of the year anymore and would often realize it had passed without my observance of it, I was spooked by the fact that the birthdays were shared. I had tried to ignore the coincidence, but it was gnawing at the edge of my consciousness, more and more as the day approached. After Angela's dubious reception of my "theory," I had avoided the subject with her, but I felt certain that there were pieces of the picture that were missing. Like I was functioning on one plane, ignoring all others, and letting atoms fall past me. They fell from the sky, from different galaxies, and kept falling, beyond my feet, beyond the earth. Should I try to catch them?

When all the kids had left, and the magazine was ready for launch, I sat down again at my computer with a half a cup of cold coffee. I pulled up a search engine and began running phrases like "Three Die April 16th" and "three girls tragedy." "April 16th, 1989 three girls die" brought up the archived Santa Cruz Post articles about Athena, Kenya and Sam, and of course me and Angela. I moved past this quickly. I had seen these articles many times before, but I was always a little startled by seeing our young faces peering at me from amid the printed material.

They had used our senior photos, which were ridiculously beautiful. They had been staged in the miniature garden behind Joe's Photography, a funny little studio on the west side; its façade was rather dingy and fronted the highway, but its tiny back yard yielded incongruously lush and bountiful foliage, fountains and concrete benches upon which to pose our anticipation of what was to come. In the photos, light edges our youthful faces, our bright, sinewy bodies, and we wear expressions of exhilaration and contentment.

The next few searches were fruitless. Then this: "Three Teens Die in Small Plane Crash." The title in bold letters floated before me on my screen. The page was dated Monday, April 16th, 1971 and had been archived by the Associated Press.

"Jesus," I whispered. It was an expletive I saved for particularly alarming occurrences. This qualified. I continued reading to find that on precisely the day of the birth of Athena, Kenya and Sam, three eighteen year old girls had died. Again, April sixteenth. I felt certain that if I kept searching, I would come up with more of these 'coincidental' birth and death dates. A pattern of eighteen years, repeating itself again and again. The implication of this pattern for my three students shot through me like lightning.

Suddenly I was covered in atoms. As if under a ton of snow. No, in a storm of atoms, all of them swirling around my ears, obscuring my vision, colliding with one another, the natural order of experience having gone haywire. "Let the atoms fall as they may," Virginia Woolf had written, but these were crashing into one another, into my body as I stood there in my classroom that night, panting my fear into life. There were no words for this fear. The collusion of fate and experience negated Confucius' claim that things don't exist until they are named. And yet I was convinced that to name this now would be disastrous. A calamity beyond naming. If only I could prevent the manifestation of this super-, this un-, this actual-reality by not speaking it. Not writing it down. No, it was already written, it seemed. I stemmed the urge to vomit by willing my body to action. I grabbed my car keys and headed for my Jeep, still in the dormitory lot.

Phyllis anticipated my arrival, having heard my Jeep screech onto the asphalt drive of Paniolo Square. She was standing in her open doorway with a concerned look on her face when I reached the landing.

"Jake, come in," she said and closed the door behind me.

"Thanks, Phyllis. I'm sorry I'm coming over so late..." It was eleven o'clock at night, but she had not been asleep. She gestured for me to sit down at a round table in what looked like a kind of breakfast nook.

"Tea?" she offered.

"Love some," I said, somewhat recovering my wits.

"Here you go," she said, handing me the already hot pot of water and a tray with various kinds of herbal and black teas. "Honey?"

"No thanks," I said, comforted by the deliberate actions of choosing a tea, unwrapping the bag, pouring water, steeping.

"Alright," I said, taking a long, deep breath. "This is a bit strange for me."

"I know, you usually have coffee, but I thought..."

Her eyes were wide and gentle. Her humour softened the moment, helped me to keep breathing. Made me feel almost sane.

"I think something terrible is going to happen," I blurted.

"Terrible," Phyllis repeated, contemplatively.

"Yes, terrible." I was looking at her searchingly, but her expression was a blank. She waited patiently for me to continue. "This weekend. On the sixteenth. I can't explain how I know this. It's so weird. I think I—"

Phyllis continued to gaze steadily at me, waiting patiently for me to sort through my thoughts, find a point of entry.

"Look," I began. "Do you believe in reincarnation? No—not reincarnation. Angels. Like spirits who take bodies in this life. Again and again. But briefly...like eighteen years."

"Just to bless the people they touch," she said softly, completing my own thought. I'm sure my mouth was agape. Not only at her unagitated response to my "wild and whirling words," but also by my own ability to articulate such ideas.

"Some people are not long for this earth, Jake," she said somberly, her tone cautionary.

"I know!" I said, encouraged by the echo of Mrs. Gates' words, which I had carried with me for so long. "That's just it!" I was fairly excited now.

"We are lucky to know them," said Phyllis, matter-of-factly. Each time she spoke, it had the effect of some soothing unction that brought down the level of intensity in the room. Like a child, I raised it quickly again each time I opened my mouth. I felt like a bull in a china cabinet, but I couldn't stop myself.

"What if we get a chance to know them twice?" I asked, barely able to contain my wayward energy.

"Do you know how unlikely that would be, Jake?" she said over her glasses. "And how unlikely, beyond that, that we'd even know it when it happened?" she continued. For the first time I noticed how much Phyllis had aged. Her eyes looked tired, and her hair had gone completely silver. Her body had diminished over time, and she looked much smaller than I had thought her to be before. Still, her irises blazed fiercely from across the table. She wanted me to hear her now, and I tried to listen.

"Yes, but—" I so wanted to believe…

"Maybe we are just meant to try and see what it is they want to teach us. Perhaps we fail if we don't manage to do this. Take what they give us, appreciate it deeply, and then move on." Phyllis quietly poured herself some more tea and, setting down the pot, brought her eyes level with mine again.

"But what if they come back?" I insisted.

"You're doubly blessed, Jake. That is all." The echo of my own favorite line: *That is all, that is all*. But could it ever be that simple?

"But I need to stop it," I said simply, and as if she had read my mind, she answered calmly.

"What, Jake? The momentum toward fate? You're going to stop that?" She looked at me now with sympathy, and I resisted her resignation to this thing she called *fate*.

"It's a waste," I said bitterly. "It's—" but I stopped myself.

"You're in love," she said simply.

"What?! No—I—she's—they're seventeen!"

"You're out of synch, Jake," she said. Again, a simple observation.

"No-I don't think you understand. It's just I can maybe stop something terrible from happening, and I think I should. If there's anything I can do, then I should do it." Phyllis could see that I was not hearing her. My heart was spinning its own circle.

"You're in a state of inertia, Jake," she said. Then she folded her hands and sat back, as if she had decided something important. "But you do what you need to do," she added.

"What do you mean a state of inertia?"

"I mean you can't see outside of the circle you're spinning. Does everything have to be either good or bad? Terrible or wonderful? Things just *are,* Jake. That's it."

"But I don't want to lose," I began, but then I checked myself, re-ordered my language. It could not be selfishness driving this whole thing, could it? "I don't want anyone to lose like that again," I amended. "If it's avoidable, I mean."

"Don't you see that you have won? Maybe twice now. If you're right, there's no way to stop it. There's no losing here. Just the blessing of…"

"…an angel," I whispered.

"It's getting late, Jake. You should go home and get some rest." She stood now, and gestured for me to do the same.

"Rest?" I said incredulously, rising. She was guiding me toward the door. Gently. Gently.

"Sweet dreams, Jake. Sweet dreams."

"Can I talk to you again?" I asked, trying to keep the desperation out of my voice.

"Can we make it during my regular hours next time?" She was smiling at me now; it was the knowing little smile I had seen a million times before. There was some comfort in that.

"Yes, of course. I'm sorry—again, I just didn't know—you seemed like a good person to—" I stuttered.

"Good night, dear. And Jake—" I paused on my way down the stairs. Phyllis spoke gravely.

"These are fragile beings. Consciousness has not caught up to them. They would be set into a tailspin if you approached them with this, do you understand?" Her eyes were blazing again, and I nodded. "You can't talk to them about this. In this reality, they are only children. Children." Her emphasis on these last words resonated, and I played them over again and again in my head as I drove home that night.

In this reality they are only children, she had said. *Consciousness has not caught up to them. Fragile beings.* The words were still tumbling inside my skull when I pulled into the lot next to the dorm. As I did, I saw Angela saying good night to Elyse and the others. She was laughing and thanking them, her little sundress flirting with her lithe body in the light of the nearly full moon. She waited on the walkway for me to catch up to her, but I resolved to wait until morning to talk to her about anything. She was the only one left, and I would risk her thinking me insane for the possibility of gaining an ally in the plan that was already taking shape in my mind. But not tonight.

Sixteen

Angela

I tried to be gentle. Understanding. Part of me thought that Jake had taken to new heights what had always been somewhat of an obsession. One that had perhaps kept him from happinesses undreamed of in his scope of awareness. One that had limited his experience and had again and again drawn his past forward and into his present—tainting it, as it were. This obsession had functioned as a veil between us; thin, transparent in places, it was an impassable membrane, and each time I had imagined it had lifted, there it was again. It was a ghost that he continually invited into that space. It was a ghost I thought he might never let go. This—now—this was extreme. And yet…

I could not deny the strangeness of the coincidence of their births. And the cycle of dying trios of eighteen-year-old girls seemed uncanny. I decided to entertain the idea, at least for the time being.

"Okay," I said, curling my legs beneath me on the couch and cradling my coffee in my hands. "So say you are right, that somehow these three spirits are here again. What's to say your will can overpower theirs?"

"What if it's *not* their will to die at eighteen? Maybe it's beyond their control," Jake suggested. His bed head that morning was extreme, but he was in earnest, so I tried to ignore it.

"Call me crazy, but I've always thought of angels as, well, pretty powerful. Fairly autonomous, you know?" I was sipping my coffee, watching Jake through the fine steam that was rising from my cup.

"Well, we're talking about a pretty unconventional idea of angels anyway, right? I mean, did you ever imagine them as high school girls?" he asked tensely.

"True," I conceded. "Did you?"

"That depends on what kind of angels we're talking about." Like that, the tension broke in waves; it was an obvious reference to a Victoria's Secret ad campaign. Jake grinned.

"God," I said. "I'm serious here."

"I'm sorry. So am I. Shit. What can I do?"

Poor thing, I thought, looking at him from the other end of the couch. He really did mean what he said, and there was real fear in his expression.

"Alright, look," I began, ever the solutions girl, ever the pragmatist. "Plan an outing. The sixteenth is a Monday, so they're probably planning on celebrating on the weekend anyway. Make it a school thing. Make sure they're on it, and keep them busy until the end of the day. How hard could it be?" I sat back, pleased with myself. Jake looked at me thoughtfully.

"You're a good friend, Angela," he said, genuinely softening.

"I know," I said. To be honest, it didn't even feel strange that I was helping to devise a plan to divert the fates of three 'angels' by sending them on a school field trip. I sipped my coffee and wondered about the way everything with Jake felt normal. Even this.

"I'm going to make some calls," he said and gave me a quick kiss on the forehead. I closed my eyes to the brush of his lips, which was quickly replaced by the bright sunlight now spilling into the room over the smooth shoulder of Mauna Kea. I sat like this for several moments, my face warmed and illuminated by the light, listening to Jake's movements in the next room. He was shuffling through papers, gathering the phone numbers he would need to make the right calls. It was his undaunted intention to prevent what he was certain was an impending end. He intended to save the lives of three young girls who reminded him of his own, younger self, and of three angels who had left us reeling in the wake of their passage, so many years ago.

That day, while Jake was busily throwing together loose ends for a spontaneous trip to the Mauna Kea Observatory Visitor's Center, I lay on the beach at Hapuna. I was half in and half out of sleep, and I let my thoughts flit inside my head and settle upon various scenes. One I recognized as the shipwreck I had explored several years before when I had learned to S.C.U.B.A. dive in Cancun with Brock. I remembered having felt cold, though the water was remarkably warm there. I remembered the sideways light that paradoxically obscured my vision into the metal hull of the boat lying on its side just sixty feet below the surface. I also remembered having recalled a particular Adrienne Rich poem I had studied in college: "Diving Into the Wreck." I had seen it anthologized many times since and knew that it was one of her most famous works.

I was diving into my own wreck now, I thought, lying there on the hot sand. With my own "book of myths." The sound of breaking waves, and a single man playing an ukulele just down the beach, limned the periphery of my dreaming. Slipping into sleep, I began to move down, as if into a watery tomb. *Here,* I thought, *I am alone.* I found myself in Rich's "body-armor of black rubber," her "absurd flippers" encumbering my feet, her "grave and awkward mask" containing my wide eyes, my nose.

For an instant I heard a child's voice, laughing, saw the sunburned legs of a tourist pass me, flicking toasty sand into the air with every step of his rubber slippers. Then again: underwater, sleep closing in around my ears.

I followed the ladder down and down, feeling the

pressure of the sea against my ribs, my pelvis. Squeezing me. "I came to explore the wreck," says Rich's poem, "The words are purposes. The words are maps." I was exploring the depths of this, the wreck of my memory: "The wreck and not the story of the wreck/ the thing itself and not the myth/ the drowned face always staring/ toward the sun."

Yes, I thought, straining against the darkness, "stroking] the beam of my lamp slowly along the flank of something more permanent than fish or weed." Then, drawing myself up alongside the hull, I used my hand to wipe the bubbles of my own breath from a round window. It took me a moment to focus on what was there, behind the tempered glass, but when I did, it was unmistakable: Jake, peering back at me from within. He looked pale, forlorn. It was the Jake of the present.

I shuddered myself awake and sat up awkwardly to find a family of Japanese tourists standing at the foot of my towel. They were all wearing dive masks on their heads, snorkels dangling absurdly next to their faces, and staring at me. I shook my head, as if to shake the dreams from my hair, and refocused. The youngest member of the family, who was already wearing his fins, took a step toward me. He smiled broadly, revealing perfectly straight teeth, and held a small camera out to me.

"Ah, yes," I said, nodding my assent. Pushing my sunglasses up into the nest of my hair, I located the family through the lens of the little camera, let it focus, and snapped the photo.

"For posterity," I said and handed the camera back to the boy, as the family made their way to the water's edge.

It was that afternoon that I met the girls. Still a bit shaken by my own dreaming, I was making my way to Jake's classroom, where we were to meet for a sunset hike. The school was backed by acres and acres of land that spilled into rainforest where one could become lost for the rest of their life. We planned to climb to the top of the hill directly behind the horse stables. Someone had placed a white cross there, and the view from that peak was legendary, according to Jake.

As I approached the English building, I could hear Hawaiian music playing. Just as I got to Jake's door, I saw that he was not inside. Instead, there were three girls wearing plumeria flowers in their hair and dancing in a line. Each had a beautiful white lei around her neck, which had suffused the air in the room with a sweet, tropical scent. The smaller, darker girl, was positioned slightly forward, so that they made a kind of triangle. The music was enchanting, and I paused in the doorway to take in the vision of the three girls moving like birds or ghosts over the hardwood floor. The tall, blond one stopped dancing as soon as she saw me and hurried to greet me. She took both of my hands in hers and drew me toward her, kissing me warmly on the cheek.

"You must be Mr. Jameson's friend!" she said. "Nice to meet you! I'm Mia, and this is Grace. And Lydia."

Each girl greeted me in turn, kissing my cheek and hugging me, as if it were the most natural thing on earth to do. I had been in Hawai'i a few days and noticed that people generally greeted one another with a hug and kiss, but most of the ones I had encountered respected my "mainland" custom of shaking hands, keeping that personal distance they knew was so valued there. Not so with these three. In fact, I found myself ushered into the room in a flurry of their bubbling energy. They explained that "Mr. Jameson" was somewhere making copies (his second job, it had appeared to me in the short time I'd been there). They were practicing a hula to be "given" to Ms. Topman whom I knew as Elyse. She was getting married in a few weeks, and it was customary for female friends to offer a hula as an expression of their support and love and well wishes.

"She's our dorm 'mom' and we're planning a wedding shower for her up in Kanehoa dorm. We're trying to practice our hula; you can help us!" It was Lydia who spoke, and her gentle touch on my arm guided me to sit on a chair that faced them where they danced.

"You be Ms. Topman," said Grace, excitedly, "and we'll dance for you." Wisps of her sun-reddened hair slipped into her eyes and out again as she brushed them away.

"Okay," I said tentatively, but their energy was delicious, their smiles too sweet to deny them anything. They quickly took their places, and Mia pushed play on a boom box near my feet. Once she was in line with the others, the music shifted, and together, they began to move. As the honeyed voice of the singer intoned the Hawaiian lyrics, Lydia spoke softly the English translation of her words.

"This is to you/ O sage blossom/ A cherished sweetheart/ That attracts the mind," she said, bringing her hand to her temple in a soft flourish that indicated the thoughts. It was a song called "Pua Lililehua," written for the wife of the composer. It was about the red sage brush flower of that name.

"While you go seeking/ Among the beauties of the land/ Right here I remain/ Waiting for your return," Lydia continued, as the bodies of the girls undulated, conveying the story of a lover waiting patiently for her beloved. I knew enough about hula to understand that it was an integral part of ancient Hawaiian culture and was used to another human being, to the divine, to communicate emotion, as well as stories. These three did all of this, their smiles and gestures directed to me, sitting there as a stand-in for Elyse. Absurdly, I felt overwhelmed with emotion, my eyes welling with tears. It was as if they *did* dance for me, the bride-to-be, and the outpouring of their love reached me through the movements of their hands, their hips, their shifting, wide-open eyes.

When the song ended, I felt tired, as if I had danced the five verses of the intensely emotional song. Each of the girls came to me in turn, put the lei from her own neck over my head, and kissed me again. With tuberose flowers beguiling my senses, I sat there blinking. I was moved not only by what could be conveyed through movement in this incredible traditional dance, but also by the hearts of the three girls who now stood before me expectantly, awaiting my response.

I was interrupted by clapping that was coming from the doorway. Jake stood there now, applauding what he had caught of their hula.

"It was lovely, girls," I said to them, immediately aware of the inadequacy of my words.

"Really?" said Mia happily.

"Really."

The girls were thrilled and quickly began to gather their things to go, not wanting to impose on my time any longer.

"Thank you for sharing that with me," I said, still a little discomposed but finding my wits again. "I loved it." I meant this, too. It wasn't something I said often…I *love* it. I didn't like the overuse of that word and avoided using it to describe my feelings toward things like particularly tasty food or superior movies. I meant it, though. I did *love* their hula. I *loved* the experience of it, how it seemed to connect me to them, as if by osmosis—some shared female sensibility. I even felt a little envious toward Elyse Topman, imagining her reception of this incredible gift, what it represented, the ceremony and life decision it connoted.

I was a little embarrassed that Jake had witnessed my rather overt display of emotion, but it was real, and that was all. The girls bustled out of the room, effusive in their thank yous and good byes, slinging bags over shoulders and giggling all the way.

"They're pretty great, huh?" asked Jake. I stiffened slightly against his praise, but only for a moment.

"What, at dancing?" I said in as detached a voice as I could muster.

"In general," he said. And it was useless to deny that I, too, had been smitten.

"Yes, they're pretty great *in general*," I conceded. In fact they had made a significant impression on me, and I felt myself wishing I could be present in three weeks to see Elyse receive her hula, be ed by the dorm girls and blessed by their wishes for a happy marriage. It came both of my attraction to these lovely little spirits and of a growing desire to be in Jake's life in a more substantial way. My flight to New Zealand left in five days, and I would be on it, I remember thinking. It was something I was doing for myself.

The aunt I was going to visit was my Aunt Sylvia, who was one of the most powerful women I had ever met. She lived alone in Raglan, but was rarely by herself, so popular was her surfside accommodation and home cooking. When I was fourteen she had made a rare foray out of Raglan to meet my family in Australia, where my parents had a photo shoot. She was my mother's sister, and they had not seen one another for years. There were long hours when my parents were working, and Auntie Sylvia and I walked along the beaches in our "togs," as she called them, talking of magical things. She believed in angels and fairies and instead of supplicating to God, she would ask the angels to guide and protect her. She collected herbal remedies and essential oils that brought healing, and she carried in her bag a whole host of crystals and stones, all of which she shared with me. She would speak to the stones and crystals, and whisper their healing secrets to me.

It was Auntie Sylvia who told me, during that trip to Australia, that I was a *healer*. I didn't know what it meant at the time and for some weeks afterward, I thought perhaps I should consider med school for a future pursuit, since I didn't want to miss my *calling*. But "way leads on to way," and I never returned to that particular juncture, where the path toward practicing medicine seemed to be at my feet and beckoning. I only carried with me from those mystical days with Auntie Sylvia her suggestion that I was a *healer,* whatever that meant, and the distant sound of the shore birds, so different from the ones I had heard elsewhere. I would extrapolate the many implications of her suggestion over the years of my life and not learn until much later that she was simply recognizing my humanity.

I have since learned that the gift of healing is in

everyone, and to recognize this in another is simply to identify one's human-ness, one's affinity toward other human beings. "Namaste," say the yogis in India and Nepal, recognizing aloud the existence of the perfect, the light, the divine in another. It is a salutation that expresses one's profound identification with that aspect of being, because in fact, it exists in oneself, too. The Hawaiians say "Aloha," and I find it to be an expression of the exact same thing. Its folk etymology claims that it unites two Hawaiian words: *alo* and *ha*. *Alo* means "presence," and *ha* means "breath of life" or "essence of life." Aloha, like namaste, is an identification with one's higher self and with the divine in another human being. It is a sharing of that "essence," and a Hawaiian "kiss" involves the exchange of that "breath of life."

Lydia, Mia and Grace had done this in the three and a half minutes of their dance; they had shared that "breath" with me. They had awakened some very small thing in me, which would have been easy to ignore and even forget had the events that followed been different. To what extent they were conscious of their gift to me, I could not say. They were children, after all, and though beautiful in their dance, still innocent. Still green. It was what came through on a less conscious level, that "ha," as it were. It was the *suggestion* of healing. Of love, as it is expressed in Hawaiian: "Aloha."

It was also that, like Jake, I could see Athena, Kenya and Sam in them. There was something I couldn't put my finger on, that perhaps I would not have noticed had Jake not pointed out the similarities. But I had to admit it. And the words that Lydia spoke and to which they moved…they had seemed to be *my* words. *My* song.

"Let's go," I finally said to Jake, still wearing my three tuberose leis. I was eager to move down, out of my head and into my body. We still had that hike to take, and we were both game for a little challenge. Jake quickly changed his shoes and we were off.

Seventeen

Jake

I was successful in putting the trip together, getting permission forms out and back again, and enticing the three girls, among about twenty-six other students, to join the fun. It was easy to put a trip together for boarders, as their opportunities for recreation, especially on a "school night," were often limited, and they had only to get the permission of their dorm parents, who could sign off their entire hall at once. I had invited Angela, but she had declined to come, feeling perhaps that it was my time with the kids, my own vigilante effort to re-channel fate, and *my* opportunity to put something to rest once and for all.

Standing at the door as I was leaving, Angela had appeared beautiful to me, radiant even. I remember wondering for a moment what it would be like to touch the skin beneath her sheer white tunic, clinging here and there to her body and the lacy white camisole that adorned it. I touched her shoulder, just barely, and she looked at me with a tiny question in her eyes. She did not give it words, though, and instead kissed me. It was not the kind of kiss she normally gave me; it lingered, and there was more of her body against mine than felt like a goodbye. I leaned into it, a little dizzy, and found myself tipping back into the room. Giggling, she pushed me back out the door and said goodbye. I could still hear her little laugh from behind the door, as I made my way down the path toward the busses.

It was a two-hour bus ride from campus to the Visitors' Center, half way up the massive, sleeping volcano. I would escort the kids, along with Elyse, who taught science, to the center, spend a couple of hours looking at the displays and viewing the night sky through the telescopes they had set up there. We'd drink hot cocoa, give our extra credit assignments and head home. My plan put us back at school around 11:30pm, just in time to send the students into their respective dorms for a good night's sleep. With Tuesday off of school for teacher in-service, the students could sleep in, and I could breathe again.

The mountain is cool, even in April, and it was fun for us to don beanies and coats, scarves and gloves, which were otherwise rarely a part of our wardrobe. Some had borrowed these things from day students, whose travel clothes were at least at their houses in town. Most of these kids, I knew, left such items at their homes in places like Michigan, Iowa and New York. It was comical to see them bundled as if for a blizzard for the colder Mauna Kea weather, to which none of us was acclimated.

An evening field trip is always an opportunity for young couples to take advantage of the chance to be away from campus and together in a less strictly monitored situation. Elyse took it upon herself to police that situation, which freed me up to peruse the various displays and find the constellation or planet upon which each display telescope was trained. The kids were milling about, taking notes in their science journals and chatting easily.

I had been deeply involved in peering through a telescope for some time, and when I pulled away from the lens, I was startled by the black irises of Lydia, very near to mine.

"Whoa, hey there!" I exclaimed, taking a step backward. "You snuck up on me!"

"Sorry, Mr. Jameson," was all she said, but she looked a little amused at my discomfort.

"Nah, hey, it's okay. Have a look," I said, gesturing toward the telescope. "It's the Andromeda Constellation." Lydia looked curious and moved toward the lens, peered inside it. She wore a lavender scarf wrapped twice around her neck and a black wool coat that brushed her knees. She looked very small and very delicate to me then. I could smell the scent of coconut in her hair.

"Wow," she said, "it's beautiful. Infinite. So much space." Coming away from the lens, she beamed at me, pleased and excited, and then turned to the small plaque that accompanied the telescope.

She read aloud, her curiosity and interest apparent in her tone: "The constellation Andromeda is in the northern sky near the constellation Pegasus. It is most notable for containing the Andromeda galaxy, an enormous spiral galaxy approximately two-point-five million light years away. It is the nearest spiral galaxy to our own, the Milky Way. The Andromeda Constellation is sometimes called the 'chained maiden' in English."

"Did you see her?" I asked. "Here," I said. "Look again."

After some time of peering into the telescope, Lydia finally exhaled. "Oh yeah," she said. "She's like a stick figure woman. Looks like she's wearing a big belt."

"That's it!" I said, happy she had been able to locate the elusive image. "And she's holding a long sword."

"Yes, I see it!" she said excitedly. "Why is she called 'the chained maiden' do you think?"

When I didn't answer her right away, she pulled back from the telescope and looked at me, her upturned face very near my chest. It was hard not to just stare at her, so open was her expression, so beautiful her face. I knew her well by now, after nearly a year of having her in class. I had read her most intimate thoughts, the delicate and sometimes haunting language she gave to them. It only took an instant for enchantment to give way to self-awareness, and I cleared my throat, stepped back from her. I sent my gaze upward, toward the black vault of sky and the stellar jewels that sparkled there.

"Well, in ancient Greek mythology, Andromeda was a virgin princess," I explained, deferring to my teacher persona. "Her father, in order to appease a terrible sea monster that was wreaking havoc on his people, was directed by the oracle to chain her to a rock as a sacrifice."

"Oh my god, that's terrible!" she exclaimed, covering her mouth rather theatrically.

"Yeah, it is," I agreed, chuckling. "She was innocent. She had no say in the matter. She was to be sacrificed to save her people."

"Well," she said thoughtfully, twirling several of the strands of her scarf's fringe, "how do we know she didn't offer herself? Maybe the oracle spoke to *her*."

"Well, Lydia, the myth tells us—"

"Mr. Jameson," she chided, "you are the first to teach us that myth is fluid and changes with the teller. How do you *know*? Maybe she *wanted* to do it. For her family…and her friends."

Her gaze on me was level, lucid, her eyes glossy and serious. She continued: "You're always saying how that's the great thing about mythologies; that we can borrow them and make them our own. Give them the details that suit our present story."

It was this last sentence that disconcerted me. "Our present story?" I asked, but her childlike response put me at ease.

"Yeah. The one we happen to be writing at the time."

This time it was I who exhaled heavily. I was visited by a swift awareness of my own absurdity, just for a moment, how I wanted to attach meaning to every syllable, every act. I had to admit I made a lousy existentialist.

"Right. Of course," I said quietly.

She seemed to get an idea, and turning toward me, spoke with considerable energy, her mittened hand resting softly on my arm. "You know," she said, "the Plains Indians believe that before we become people in this life, we are nearly perfect. Spirit. Light. Floating around out there."

She waved her little hula hand in the direction of the stars and continued. "All we are lacking is the experience of limitation. So we take a body on this earth to experience limits."

"And therefore become truly perfect and whole," I offered.

"Yes! You've heard of this," she said, surprised.

"Yeah, the Sun Dance religion."

"Exactly."

Her surprise at my knowledge of the Sun Dance religion smarted a bit, and I teased her: "What, you think my knowledge is limited to literature?" I whined.

"No, I—" She looked genuinely concerned for a minute, and I knew I should probably not have joked like that. It had never ceased to amaze me how someone so figurative with her language in poetry could be so literal in life, but so it was with Lydia.

"I'm just teasing you," I said, nudging her with my elbow. "Besides, I did learn it through literature, actually. *Seven Arrows* by—"

"Hyemeyhosts Storm!" she said eagerly, easily distracted from her fear of insulting me.

"Yeah," I said. "Wow." I had not met very many teenagers who had read Storm's work, save those to whom I had introduced it. I was just getting ready to ask how she knew it, when our conversation was interrupted by Elyse, already rounding up the kids for the ride home. She wanted to make it home by midnight, she said.

"Of course," I had said, straightening and beginning to assist in herding students toward the busses, reminding them to make a last stop at the restrooms before boarding. I remember feeling ethereal, light, as if I myself were made of stars. The combination of my conversation with Lydia and the anticipation of my success in diverting her imminent demise, real or imagined, seemed to serve as an elixir. I was elated, insubstantial…floating again.

When we arrived on campus, we let the girls off the

bus first, outside Kanehoa Dormitory.

"Okay, ladies!" I exclaimed. "We've made it home. Up and attem'!" Many of them had fallen asleep, and they were now looking a little disoriented, rubbing their eyes and gathering their things. "Make sure you check in with the on-duty person. They are expecting you." As Mia, Grace and Lydia made their way down the aisle, I could see that they were sleepy and happy to be home.

"Thanks, Mr. Jameson! It was awesome," said Mia drowsily.

"Happy Birthday, girls," I said.

"Hey, you remembered!" exclaimed Grace.

"Of course I remembered," I said, mussing her hair roughly.

"The big party is tomorrow night, though. You're still invited, you know," reminded Lydia, looking at me with her head cocked to the side. Grace's aunt lived in Waimea and was hosting a huge luau for the three of them.

"Yeah, I think I'll give that one a pass. I do like my job," I said.

"Yeah, we don't want to get you fired just yet!" laughed Grace. "Wait till we graduate!"

"Good night, girls. Get some sleep, okay?" I tried to keep the pleading out of my voice.

"Of course, Mr. Jameson," said Mia reassuringly.

As Lydia passed me, she put her hand on my chest, as if to touch my heart. The expression she gave me was untranslatable and could have meant anything.

"Good night, Lydia."

She smiled at me over her shoulder as she descended the steps of the bus. It was such a little girl's smile. There was mischief there, and happiness. That is all. *That is all.*

"Next stop, boys' dormitory!" I bellowed, and the driver closed the great yellow door and moved us along to our final destination.

When I finally entered my apartment, it was nearly

midnight. I felt pleased with myself and finally empty of the fear that had filled my heart for so many weeks. I had kept the girls out until nearly midnight. They were obviously exhausted from the day's events and would crawl into their beds now, safely beyond the ill-fated day, dreaming of tomorrow's birthday festivities. I had kept them from perpetuating the cycle of untimely death. Without knocking them out of their child sensibilities, without shattering the glass between dimensions or crossing some invisible line between the super-real and the real, I had altered their course. I had opened up before them…life. I felt unspeakably powerful and profoundly peaceful at the same time.

Angela was sleeping in my bed, one leg thrown out from the duvet to reveal a slender calf, her gently arching foot. Without thinking about it, I took off jeans and sweater and slid into bed behind her, cradling her in the hollow I made with my body. She made a small sighing sound and nestled in to me, as if we had done that every night for our whole lives. I fitted my chin in the space between her ear and her shoulder, breathing her lavender and lemongrass scent. I was home. The girls were safe. I felt I could sleep.

Some hours later, I was awakened as if by a huge jolt. I sat bolt upright in the bed, having thrown the covers off. I was breathless and afraid, as if I had been having a bad dream, but I could remember nothing.

Angela sat up, too, and put her hand on my chest, where my heart was beating madly and erratically, it seemed.

"You okay?" she asked, concerned. Her eyes were soft and deep, the of sea grass. She moved her hand from my heart to my face, traced my jaw with her fingers. I allowed myself to be soothed by Angela, though something stirred in my ribcage still. I closed my eyes, felt myself begin to float downward, toward soil so rich it looked like a night sky bejeweled with tiny mineral stars.

"Yeah," I said. "I think so." I felt drawn down into my body, my shimmering, insubstantial self merging with its fleshy, material counterpart.

When I turned to face her, I saw that her irises swam in the pools of her eyes, sea grass swirling there inside star-like hoops of gold. Angela had never let go of her tender grasp on my fingertips. She had been holding ground for both of us for what seemed like a lifetime: gallant and smiling, the ethereal edifice of our longing rising in the distance like a pale pink church on green hills.

I let my hand find her body then. Barely touching her, I traced her breasts with my fingertips, began to learn her; I traced along her neck and cradled her head in my hand, burying my fingers in her kelp-ed hair. I took a handful of it, drew her face gently to mine. Angela's kiss on my mouth then felt like opening myself up to the warm cave of my own desire.

Touching her I felt the buzz of our combined energies, the magnet of one soul against another. Gravity doing its job for a change. We made love slowly, each breath completing something that seemed to have begun in ancient times, before these bodies. Before fire. Before air. When there was only water. We were liquid, moving in the fluid substance of our want—two capable of a shattering union. A unifying explosion of self. Sighs. Utterances of every sacred syllable effecting the dissolution of what made us separate, had kept us apart until that moment.

I fell asleep tangled in her hair, in my desire for her, and in a kind of serenity that was wholly new to me. I settled into the sweet heaviness a body can have. I never knew.

Eighteen

Angela

Our bliss was short lived. I remember lying there in Jake's arms, savoring his scent, his pulse. His knees lined the backs of mine. My hips were tucked in to the nest of his body. Before the room had taken on the daylight, we could hear activity in the hallway outside Jake's door. It was an unpleasant buzz. There was a speed to the movement and sound that alarmed us both, and Jake was on his feet in moments, struggling to put on his jeans and see what was the matter.

I think I knew in my heart, which compressed itself in the cavern of my chest, as I listened to the anxious, distraught tones of Jake's voice from the hall, the voices of the others who moved there. It seemed inadmissible. It seemed extraordinary that any of what Jake had imagined could be real. Actual. But it was.

When Jake had come in from the hall and then gone again, his stricken face hung before me like a mask. I had buried myself in the covers, so that only my eyes were visible. I had sunk into a deep sleep of avoidance, knowing it was not me that Jake sought to guide his frantic struggle to piece together the previous night's events. I had been in this position with him before. It was an ironic and inconceivable repetition of our history.

He would be swept up in the currents of other mourners and finally devoured by his own grief. This I knew. And there was the element of blame; again, my nebulous hand in the twist of fate that had allowed such a thing to occur. Indeed, what happens simultaneously is inextricably linked in our sensibilities. It is a flaw of human conception. I could not expect Jake to be able to extract our union from the destruction and chaos that had swallowed our love as soon as it was born. I anticipated his limits. I made it easy for him.

When he came home, I was ready to leave. He had been gone most of the day. I imagined him comforting students, explaining to families, consoling himself in the rare moments he found himself alone. He had not checked in with me, and I did not expect him to. I was a guest to this life of his, and when such a life is violated so powerfully, it is stripped down to the core. All flesh melts away, and bone clings to bone, grateful for the simplicity of a skeletal state. I was completely packed when he arrived at seven that night. We had only to give ourselves over to a dreamless sleep, perhaps once more in a shared bed, and I would leave him to re-order his life, which certainly he would choose to do alone, with his many ghosts.

Nineteen

Jake

How many times have I tried to reconcile myself to the anachronism of children dying before their parents? Of a young body stripped of life. A family stripped of its joy. I don't know how we live through it, really. I first learned from the Gateses and the Hawthornes. I saw Mrs. Gates build a little shrine to her girl, saw her diminish physically, until her skin was little more than a fine tissue that might tear or disintegrate in a too hot bath. She would cup her small breasts in her hands, lying in darkness on her bed, whispering prayers that got lost somewhere between her languid body and the ceiling. Her husband would close the door quietly against this image, this shell of his wife. He simply accepted the job of going on. Someone had to be alive for Camille, who more and more appeared as Athena in miniature. I don't know if this made it easier or more difficult to bear her absence.

Somehow I was not surprised when I woke to find that they were gone. Mia, Lydia and Grace had slipped out of their dorm within minutes of "lights out." They had ambled down the grassy hill below Kanehoa dormitory, their figures gently lit by a full-bellied moon. They had jaunted through campus secretly and descended the next level of green hillside, their pale garments lifting from their bodies like wings, their voices ringing like bells in the night air. I invent the image, of course. Even the sound is borrowed from my memory of Athena's voice.

Their destination was Mikela Johnson's Lexus, parked across the two-lane highway. It was left with its keys under the driver's floor mat for the express purpose of transporting the birthday girls to the party at Kohala Ranch. Clever. The day students and others who had signed out for the long weekend would already have been there, overindulging, blowing off the pressure of another week where every single minute is structured for them. They would have been laughing, light-headed perhaps, at intervals peering down the long drive lined with pine trees for the headlights that would never appear there.

The roads on the Big Island are dark. Driving at night on its highways, one feels as though he is a lone S.C.U.B.A. diver in a vast sea, zooming along the ocean floor with his own dive lamp as the only light in an inviolable darkness. At any significant speed, one is surprised even by an ordinary curve in the road. I don't know what happened exactly. There had been many accidents on that road and others over the years. We had been lucky enough not to lose any students this way in my tenure at H.I.A., but now…Now.

I managed to put my own grief at bay for some time, and more than ever I belonged to my students. When Angela said she was going, I understood it as her way of allowing me to give myself to my students in this way. She was not abandoning me, though I would have liked nothing more than to keep her with me. She had a distance to travel, too, and this was *my* loss. *My* grief to navigate. It seemed I had pulled her into my personal spirals, or kept her outside of them, enough in our lives already. I acknowledged her love and her friendship, let her go for the time being.

Heeding Elyse's advice to "feed their sadness," I made pot after pot of chili, soup, stew…whatever I could make and keep hot for the kids to put in their bellies as they sat around my apartment, glassy eyed and somber. They said very little; some of the boys slept on my couch or on my floor, not wanting to return to their dormitory rooms. After the initial shock, where I found myself trying to catch their gangly limbs as they collapsed into heaps of elbows and knees, tears burning in their round eyes, the experience became like a long pantomime of anguish and finally, of exhaustion.

The edges blurred—of days and scenes, and even words. We moved through hours, memorial services, the ritualistic locating of a place on campus to pile with our mementos, our flowers, our sadness. *Everyone* felt their loss, their haunting absence.

Students said things to me like, "Really? They're not just late coming back to campus? They're really not coming?" It was Max Le'ahi.

"No, Max. They're not coming back." His incredulous expression broke my heart and seemed to beg me to take it back.

"Never?" he asked.

"Never," I said, my own heart filling with the whole picture that had begun to take shape as early as my seventeenth year in life. My own heart rejecting the words I spoke.

The services were eerily familiar, the pews of the rustic campus chapel filled with kids who had loved the girls, who had admired them, met them once or not at all. It is all grief. Every variety of it legitimate. The grief of the mother. The grief of the girl who left the keys under the mat. Of the boy who sat next to Lydia in AP Biology and never spoke her name. Of the girl who opted not to go on the Observatory field trip and ride in the Lexus with them; she was holding a sweating beer bottle in her hand and laughing softly when they heard the distant sound of the screeching tires, the ensuing crash, far off and muffled by trade winds. She had cocked her head, thought she heard something, then dismissed it as her imagination.

Real, too, is the grief of the child who realizes because of these strangers to himself, that he too will expire—one day be without breath. Without life. And then there was the grief of me, the man who had loved a shade for most of his life and tried to save her from the transformation that was always happening. Always there had been her arrival, always her departure.

It was in Waimea Java that I met up with Phyllis again. Still mired in the corporeal, I had gone over and over the details in my head. In my limited perspective, it had seemed almost formulaic to me: a calculated string of events that might blast the course of fate.

"I kept them busy until eleven thirty at night," I said. "I didn't imagine they had plans to sneak out of the dorm. Though I don't know why I didn't think of it." Phyllis' grey eyes seemed to swirl and gather like rain clouds above the rims of her glasses, and her silver hair glistened beneath the recessed lights of the coffee house. I was aware of these things, and the veins on the backs of her wiry hands, as I spoke. Another friend moving, more slowly perhaps, toward a departure, I remember thinking. God I was morose.

"Jake," she said simply.

"I don't understand it," I continued. I wanted to get to the bottom of something. To keep turning the soil until it appeared. Something material and satisfying.

"I see," was her response, and she took a sip of her tea, leveled her gaze upon me again.

"What's that supposed to mean?" I asked. To me, her words contained a judgment, and I wanted to understand it. I trusted her, believed in her, but I still felt defensive.

"Well, it's how you see things. In terms of their departures, not in terms of their presence. What you experience, what is given to you, *that* is real. Not what is gone. Once it's gone, it's gone, but you will always have what you remember. What they taught you. *That* is real."

"Like Tara," I said simply, remembering Angela's little figurine. Her gift to me.

"The goddess?"

"Yeah," I said, pulling it out of my pocket. I couldn't remember when I had started to carry it with me. I closed my hand around it, then, and Phyllis closed her hand around mine. She seemed to read my mind.

"Angels come in many forms," she said gently. I became suddenly hyper-aware of my self-indulgence.

"I must sound really ungrateful," I said with real shame.

"I think angels are pretty understanding," she said. She stood then and gave me one of those ambiguous winks. So much meaning was contained therein, I knew. I also knew that it might be a long while before I grasped it fully. In the meantime I was grateful for Phyllis' friendship and for her willingness to listen without judgment. I told her so.

"You're a good boy, Jake," she said. It was simple. Something you might say to a dog. Or a child. But it soothed me, reassured me, and I believed her. Perhaps not in my actions or even in my words. But in my intent. Perfect. I *was* good. *I was good.*

After comforting the kids for weeks, I hardly had the energy to grieve myself. For what I had lost—twice. It was hard for me. As prepared as I must have been, having conceived, before it even happened, of the possibilities of divine intention, I still felt like I was standing in a vacuum. It was as if a great wind had moved violently past my body, taking with it some vestige of an ancient faith. It had sucked all the air from the space I occupied, left me alone: diminished, hollow. Some crazy urgency would rise in my ribcage, my flaccid heart, at intervals—make me feel I had missed a window of opportunity. For what, I do not know. To change the course of fate? To communicate something to the spirit that was undoubtedly that very one to whom I had attached myself so early in life, continued to pine after in the secret places of my soul and in my writing? Perhaps. Perhaps.

In this reality they are only children, Phyllis had said. *Children.* I had had a responsibility to the child that was Lydia. I knew that. I had ed that, hadn't I? But then I would be devoured again by my self-indulgent grief, my sense of injustice. My belief that it could have been somehow different. In my heart I knew it could not have been. There was no way to envision a relationship to a girl I knew as someone else. As occupying a different body, with a different set of memories. A different conception of the world.

It was not that I had hoped to share a life with Lydia, nearly eighteen years my junior. I knew her as a girl. My star poetry student. I had never allowed my imagination to take me beyond the breathless moments of connection I felt in hearing her poems, the seconds I thought I saw a glint of recognition in her deer-like eyes. Never had I touched her face, her hair. She had touched *me,* deeply, had visited me in the ether of our shared humanity. *That is all.*

One night in May, I dreamt I was outside my apartment, among the trees that stood there like a veil between me and the physical world. I moved like light, like a dragonfly or, and the image strikes me even now as absurd, as if riding one of those imperial speed bikes from Star Wars. I moved through the trees so fast, almost faster than the eye could follow, so that there trailed behind me the residue of my own image, itself appearing like gold light or glitter. Fairy dust, even. Athena was there. Lydia. So were the other girls. We were seven, we were four. Light. Energy. Unencumbered by the "mortal coils" of our bodies.

We knew each other intimately, but there was no

great emotion other than to enjoy our unhindered movement. To revel in the uninhibited nature of the life force that was there for us all; we drew from it, as from a well, let it carry us along an invisible timeline, a river of self and other and some connective fluid: ether or, could it have been? Love.

There is a group of people called the Bahais, whose elders answer quite simply the question of what holds the atom together in its infinite inertia, its electrons circling the neutron endlessly. Unselfconsciously, they answer. Without fear. It is *love,* of course, say the sages of this tradition. Simply. Of course. *Of course.*

When I woke from this dream, my grief had broken like a wave upon the shore. It had dispersed, like so much water, so much foam, across the stones, whispering *sssshhhhhh,* as it receded into the sea. My consciousness, too, receded, and I was again immersed in sleep. I saw, as if from hovering above my body: myself floating. I felt so strange, a foreigner in my own edemic body, far out at sea. Bobbing at the surface. *To live even one day is so dangerous,* said Woolf's Mrs. Dalloway, and I recognized it as the song that had lived me for these many years. *Dangerous. Dangerous.* A resounding threat. An echo of a promise. A yes. This undoing. Me. I came undone. Out on the sea, I unraveled, disclosed what I was to a hostile jury of gulls, poised mid-flight and hovering over what they did not know and could not guess.

I am a shambles, I observed, but this was nothing new. And then, inexplicably, I felt myself slowly merge with that hoped-for union of selves. All of us changed, molecularly attuned. Water. Ocean. My mistress, my self. And I heard myself ask, unselfconsciously, without self-loathing or judgment: *What can I be but this thing that remains? What can I be but this*?

When I found Lydia's last poem, I had it in me only to weep. Let the sadness I had shared with so many for the past few weeks move through me like a warm breeze. It was in her journal, the one with her name written in her sprawling, loopy hand on the cover, the "a" of *Lydia* ending in a wild and continuous spiral. It was dated April 12th, 2007:

> *I cling to star and star—celestial monkey bars.*
> *I obstruct the sun's light with my own*
> *blazing body.*
> *Afire, I am set afire. I consider the irony of light*
> *casting shadow, mine cast on the moon,*
> *twirling mass*
> *of self and this unruly flame. I am the thing*
> *behind the icon lurking. This shapeless infinity*
> *that fills the ears when we sleep to dream.*
> *Good bye*
> *for now, says the angel. Good bye.*

"Good bye," I whispered back to Lydia. To Athena. To every illusion I had carried with me about what we lose, what we keep. It was all with me. It *was* me. I was light inside of flesh. I was alive, after all. I had known angels, I considered. I knew one now. She moved around the earth in a body I had known for years. My whole life, it seemed. And I had loved her, through it all perhaps. She inhabited the flesh I recognized, the flesh I had known with my own flawed body. It had been this angel who had waited, with her hand lifted into the air, keeping a light hold of my fingertips while I waved in the sky like a flag, a kite, a banner of super-reality, hovering above the earth. Inert. She had waited for me on the green hills of our shared experience, the rose-ed structure of our potential shimmering in the distance. I realized…I loved her so much it felt like hurt.

Our community was a wreck and, like my own graduation had been so many years before, this one was a pale, anemic version of the celebration it might have been. Alongside the effort to acknowledge the accomplishments of the graduating students, there were ceremonies to , remember, share. All the ways we try to process and masticate the indigestible, the un-real. Amid balloons and the tradition of lei piled high enough to impair the wearer's vision, there were the benign smiles of resignation, sympathy, even disbelief. All the ways our faces conveyed the unrest in our listless hearts as we shuffled along among the outward symbols of what one anticipates, for a lifetime perhaps, as a joyful occasion.

When it was over, and the boarders had taken the last boxes and scraps from their rooms, driven away with their parents to airports and distant towns on the island, there was only one thing left for me to do. I, too, packed my things.

Twenty

Angela

When I first came over those hills at sunset, driving a frighteningly small rental car on the left side of the road, I knew I was coming home. The fullest answer to that first question was reflected in the green hills, the darkening sky that dove into the ocean before me, and in the lights of Raglan town, just beginning to twinkle on. It was a question raised by my earliest experience of guilt, grief, untimely death.

I once read that when we sleep, our spirits are free to roam. While our bodies are anchored to the earth by their sheer weight, their *real*-ness, our spirits remember how to *be*. They lift off like impish little sprites and go travelling sometimes, though we never remember, or if we do we think we have had a marvelous dream. In that state of freedom from the body, the spirit is likely not bound by time and space the way we would be in our waking lives, not limited as we are by the corporeal.

This is the closest thing I've found to an explanation for déjà vu. We remember the scenes we have visited in our spirit forays into the timeless, limitless realm of the super-real, as Jake called it, but only vaguely. They are like layered little still images that don't reconnect once the conscious mind gets a hold of them. Though we strain against the discontinuity of these two aspects of the self, try to recall what seems irrecoverable and is finally dismissed as a fluke of the mind's erratic reels. It's the closest thing I've found to an explanation for what I am about to describe.

As I was coming over those green hills, and the crescent of glistening water that cradles Raglan came into view, I felt the air to be populated with the divine. The purely light. In my mind's eye, I saw three sleeping babies, somewhere in the world, soft, perfect in their infant dreaming. I saw them as little seeds awaiting the angelic bloom of purpose in their lives. Three little girls, the ancient knowledge of their departures already written in their hearts and secretly, in the hearts of their mothers, who cried when they were born. They thought they were crying because the pain had ended, because the long wait was over, or because of the infinite beauty expressed in the tiny forms of the babies they bore. But they were not crying for any of these things. They were crying because somewhere in the recesses of their limitless souls there slept the knowledge that one day, in some way, they would have to let their babies go.

Nowhere is this *knowing* captured more beautifully and more intensely than in the multitude of images of the Madonna. Always in her face, the same expression: the tiny smile of resignation, too hurt to laugh or even to cry. Here, in her arms: innocence. Perfection. The infant bloom of sacrifice.

Michelangelo's last work remains unfinished. It is the Pieta Rondanini and it stands in the Villa Borghese in Rome. It is the aging Mary and her dying son. In this statue, her grief is mild, contained. It is a practiced anguish. She folds herself around him as he collapses—the culmination of thirty-three years of anticipation. What she must have agreed to, the embryonic promise still swelling in her belly—*Yes,* she must have said, and *please*. This Mary, in the Pieta Rondanini, does not weep or tear at her hair. Her jaw is set, but she will not gnash her teeth tonight. There is some kind of betrayal in indulging her grief like that. She and the man collapsing into her arms, her child-man—it is impossible to tell whether they are emerging out of stone…or being swallowed by it. Michelangelo rests too peacefully now for us to ever know. *My son, my love,* croons Mary softly, softly, and her love becomes the whisper that moves along his pale temple and spills down over our heads: compassion of the feminine divine. La Virgen de Guadalupe. Tara. Kuan Yin. Pele. Lakshmi. The list is long. These are the mothers.

As I pulled onto Bow Street, I saw people milling about with saltwater still drying in their hair; sipping "flat whites" across from one another in the cafés; chattering happily with bundled babies; walking arm-in-arm with sweatered elders, their ears cauliflowered from playing too much rugby as young men.

The air around *my* ears swirled with the angels I had known, perhaps as their seedling bodies slept, wrapped like little cocoons and nestled into dreamy cradles somewhere on the earth. They whispered to me of the kind of love that stays. They whispered to me of how every one of their mothers would have made the same choice again and again. To have and to lose, because the having, the *having*…was so utterly beautiful.

The answer is yes. It is worth it to give oneself to another, even with the kind of abandon a mother gives herself to her child. *Especially* with that kind. We are so hurt in so many ways. "We would give anything for what we have," says the poet, and when it comes down to it, we do.

With this acquiescence, this profound acceptance of *what is,* I immersed myself again in the sea. I spent most of my time in or on the water in Raglan and again, I let it heal me. Let it wash over my head and bathe me out of my weariness. It embraced me with abandon. It moved inside me like the fluid desire that had lived me all those years. This element was my lover, too. Another thing I shared with Jake. Another irony and another comfort. I loved him still.

Twenty-one

Jake

When I first drove over those green hills that tuck Raglan into its haven between the sea and estuary and provide the inland backdrop for what is arguably the most beautiful place on earth, I knew I was home. It was not only because I knew Angela was there, though of course that had infinite bearing on my sensibility. It was a primal connection to that particular bit of earth, that particular corner of an island in the vast Pacific Ocean. Years of living in Hawai'i, New Zealand's sister island chain, had given me an appreciation for island life and Polynesian culture. It had grown in me roots, which made it possible to live on such a small bit of earth and not consider myself tethered or limited. It had taught me to love the sea and consider it an indispensable part of living.

Driving the ten miles out to Whale Bay from town, I watched as the coastline wound itself southward, the wildness of *Whaingaroa* spilling off in rounded stones, grassy hills and sandy expanses, to the sea. The ocean churned in the New Zealand autumn, the powerful energy of the impending winter building beneath its surface, blooming in long, frothing waves that connected across whole bays to the delight of surfers just making their way to the breaks. Lady Karioi, the thickly wooded mountain that looks like a reclining woman, rose to the southeast, the light wind undulating the trees there to simulate her gentle breath, the rhythmic rise and fall of her chest.

When I saw Angela at the water's edge, she was crouching with her arms resting loosely across her knees, her bare feet rooted to the volcanic stone that had, over the eons, become smooth and now appeared to rise up around her. She wore a wool sweater, the kind the old fishermen in town wore. Her hair escaped a loose ponytail in soft tendrils that caught the light of the late afternoon sun, just making its way down the western sky. Perfectly still with her spine tall like a yogi, she fairly shimmered in my perception.

In my mind, I had moved like this, toward her small figure here, a million times. The image had suffused my thoughts as I had prepared to leave Hawai'i and make my way to her. I moved toward her now peacefully, the full expression of my love rising again, wavelike, in my chest.

She barely stirred when she saw me over her shoulder and instead received me with her body. I crouched behind her, encompassed her with my own body, rooted myself, too, to the rock upon which she was perched. I settled my head into the soft and familiar space between her ear and her shoulder, let my face rest against her, closed my eyes and breathed her. I was home. I was born.

The wheel of my inquietude had touched down, gained traction on the rich soil of Raglan and had already begun to move us forward into a shared future. I suppose to the casual onlooker that day, we might have looked like we were emerging from that stone upon which we crouched. Or perhaps like we were being swallowed by it. We were an unfinished work, and this was a beginning. After so many ends, a beginning.

Together we agreed to all the ways life might move in us, to all the risks involved in loving someone this deeply. In future years that agreement would manifest itself in children: miraculously our shared selves birthed into the world as two little boys who could shame us with their beauty, their honesty, their unfettered love. We would love them with the fierceness of the dying, for who among us is not dying every moment? With every movement, every thought.

No one could assure us that anything was lasting, that we would not be crushed one day by their disappearance into the super-real. But we had decided ages before, there, on that rock at Whale Bay, that it was worth the leaving. Whoever would be departing, whoever staying, everything between the wet, glistening birth of selves and the pale cast of death, was worth it. We had agreed to it all, knowing that it was the only thing we could do. *What could we be but this thing that remained? What could we be but this?*

Book Club Discussion Questions
for Kim Cope Tait's *Inertia*:

1. Cope Tait makes reference early on to "the first question" and returns to the concept in the final pages of the novel. What is "the first question," and what, ultimately, is her character's answer to that question?
2. Is *Inertia* a novel about reincarnation? Angels? Spirit guides? Try to encapsulate what Cope Tait suggests about the young female characters in her novel (Kenya, Sam, Athena; and Mia, Grace, Lydia).
3. Are Mia, Grace and Lydia aware of their unique roles in Jake's life? What is Phyllis' take on this subject?
4. Cope Tait clearly chooses the title *Inertia* for its relevance to the story on multiple levels. Name some of those levels and discuss the symbolic and actual meanings of the title with regard to each.
5. Through the lens of what is ultimately a love story, and from two different perspectives, Cope Tait explores the experience of losing loved ones, specifically *young* loved ones. What are the end results of this exploration? Does she offer any answers? Any reasoning for such life experiences?
6. Revisit Jake's poem to Athena, presented in the end of Chapter 4, and consider its meaning in light of Jake's suggestion that "in a way it is [a love poem]. It's like I wrote it for myself. For today."
7. What is the effect of having two different first person narrators? The choice is stylistic and has been employed by many writers (Faulkner, Woolf and, more recently, Kingsolver, to name a few).

Why do you think Cope Tait makes this choice for *Inertia*?

8. Revisit Adrienne Rich's poem "Diving Into the Wreck," which Tait's character Angela references heavily in Chapter 16. In what ways is Angela's trip to Hawai'i the enactment of "diving into [her] own wreck"? What are the symbolic implications of the poem and, specifically, of seeing Jake's face "peering back at [her] from within"?

9. What are the questions that *Inertia* raises for you? Have you had experiences in your life where you felt like the *super-real* and the *real* were intertwined in some way? Moments when you paused and wondered if you hadn't just felt the "ethereal traces of one who [had] gone from [you]"?

ABOUT THE AUTHOR

Inertia is Kim Cope Tait's first novel. Her other novels include *Bend the Blue Sky* and *Kealaula*. Kim's poetry and prose have appeared in literary journals and magazines in New Zealand, the U.S., and the U.K. She has a published chapbook of poems called *Element* (Leaping Dog Press) and a full length collection of poetry called *Shadow Tongue* (Finishing Line Press). Kim earned her MFA in Writing at the Vermont College of Fine Arts in Montpelier and has lived in Hawai'i, Switzerland, Colorado, California and Vermont. She now lives with her family in New Zealand.

www.ingramcontent.com/pod-product-compliance
Ingram Content Group UK Ltd.
Pitfield, Milton Keynes, MK11 3LW, UK
UKHW042020190726
13854UKWH00005B/2382